PRAISE FOR

NO ONE EVER ASKED

The Untold Story of a Civil Rights Worker

"The civil rights movement had many well-known champions, including Martin Luther King, Jr., John Lewis, and Rosa Parks. *No One Ever Asked*, however, explores how an overlooked Philadelphia college student and other forgotten foot soldiers of her generation upended their lives in the 1960s to register Georgia and Mississippi voters and to fight for racial equality. An informative, well-researched book, *No One Ever Asked* recovers a lost narrative and sheds new light on that era's grassroots campaigns to protect civil rights."
—**U.S. Senator Amy Klobuchar**

"Many authors have written about leaders of the civil rights movement, but in *No One Ever Asked* Arnold Rochvarg provides the powerful story of his cousin, Iris Geller, a white female college student dedicated to the cause of racial justice. Geller's total commitment to the movement results in the story of a compelling journey, one that reflects courage, sacrifice, frustration, and ultimately reaffirmation. Her story includes her role as a voting-rights activist, occupier of an Air Force base, and partner in an intimate interracial relationship with a fellow SNCC member. This book provides a newly revealed account about the civil rights movement from the ground up: We should all be grateful that someone finally asked Iris Geller to tell it."
—**Michael Higginbotham**, author of *Ghosts of Jim Crow: Ending Racism in Post-Racial America*

"A careful and loving recreation of a lost family story bound up with the civil rights movement. Highly readable, Arnie Rochvarg's work digs deep into the details of the civil rights struggle and his cousin's story that remained hidden from his family for decades. Rochvarg is not just a family detective but a fine writer of history—binding the two stories together. A must read for those interested in the struggle for racial equality in this nation."
—**James David Robenalt**, presidential historian, attorney, and author of *Ballots and Bullets: Black Power Politics and Urban Guerrilla Warfare in 1968 Cleveland*

"*No One Ever Asked* tells an unforgettable story of quiet courage. In 1964 Iris Geller was a young Jewish college student from Philadelphia carrying a banner in support of racial equality. By 1965 she had defied her parents, leaving home to join the fight. Her path took her to Atlanta, Savannah, and Americus, Georgia,

and finally to Columbia, Mississippi, where she worked to register Black voters and lived in the Nathan Street Freedom House, which had been recently firebombed. Her story illuminates the experience of the men and women in the civil rights struggle who put their bodies in peril on behalf of their convictions. Retired law professor Arnold Rochvarg was the first person in the family to ask his cousin Iris about those years. In telling her story and providing astute historical context, Rochvarg has rescued his cousin from oblivion and given us the book, the historical canopy, that her courage deserves."
—**Laura Kalpakian**, author of *Memory into Memoir: A Writer's Handbook*

"Iris Geller, a Philadelphia college sophomore ignited in part by the tragic murders in 1964 Mississippi of three young civil rights workers, joined a movement that changed the nation. In *No One Ever Asked,* Arnold Rochvarg vividly recounts his cousin Iris's passionate and controversial decision to leave all she had known to go on a 'years' long' journey to join the fight for a more just society and the long-term personal outcome of that consequential choice."
—**José Anderson**, author of *Genius for Justice: Charles Hamilton Houston and the Reform of American Law*

"With *No One Ever Asked,* Arnold Rochvarg delivers a captivating story, full of historical facts, that gives one a great sense of a young, determined woman living out her values."
—**Cassandra Jones Havard**, Joseph F. Rice School of Law, University of South Carolina

"Societal progress often happens only through struggle and sacrifice. In *No One Ever Asked: The Untold Story of a Civil Rights Worker*, Arnold Rochvarg—a retired lawyer and law professor—harnesses his considerable investigative skills and encyclopedic knowledge of American history to tell a never-before-told story. It is, first and foremost, about the lives that were changed and upended by the personal commitments of college students in the 1960s to travel to the segregated South—often at great risk to themselves and to the familial bonds that sometimes broke down in the face of their choices. In telling the story of Iris Geller, who, in the summer of 1965, left behind a quiet collegiate life in Philadelphia to volunteer for a voter registration drive organized by the Southern Christian Leadership Conference, Rochvarg reveals the human cost of social change as well as the risks and rewards of risking it all—for the right to vote, to organize, and to love in the days before *Loving v. Virginia* (1967), the U.S. Supreme Court case striking down laws banning interracial marriage as unconstitutional."
—**John Bessler**, author of *The Birth of American Law: An Italian Philosopher and the American Revolution*

NO ONE EVER ASKED

NO ONE EVER ASKED

The Untold Story of a Civil Rights Worker

Arnold Rochvarg

UNIVERSITY OF MISSOURI PRESS
Columbia

Published by the Curators of the University of Missouri
University of Missouri Press, Columbia, Missouri 65211
Printed and bound in the United States of America
 First printing, 2025.

Library of Congress Control Number: 2025029902

ISBN 9780826223418 (hardcover : alk. paper)

∞™ This paper meets the requirements of the
American National Standard for Permanence of Paper
for Printed Library Materials, Z39.48, 1984.

Typefaces: Minion and Trade Gothic

In Memory of My Parents, Bea and Gil

Dedicated to
My wife Ria, daughters Courtney and Molly, and granddaughter Melody
And to all those who believe in
Justice, Equality, Compassion, and the Rule of Law.

CONTENTS

FOREWORD

THE HEBREW WORD *ZAKHOR* declares the Jewish imperative to remember those who have gone before. Arnold Rochvarg has committed a significant act of love, honor, and remembrance in writing his cousin Iris Geller's long-hidden story of seven years in the 1960s civil rights movement. As Rochvarg notes, too many people and their untold stories have already been lost. Even the more well known narratives are vulnerable to recent efforts to suppress the teaching of African American history and destroy the institutions dedicated to preserving it.

In the last few years, Movement giants like Bob Moses, John Lewis, and Julian Bond have passed, as well as revered African American women leaders like Gloria Richardson, Bernice Johnson Reagon, and Dorie Ladner. They barely get the attention they deserve except in civil rights veteran circles. Even more vulnerable to being forgotten are the stories of ordinary, extraordinary foot soldiers, those who made sacrifices every day on the front lines. Local African American people are living out their days in small southern towns, still facing ongoing, if more subtle, inequalities. Women civil rights veterans, who often played less visible yet vital roles, still cherish their Movement work and remain actively committed to change. Many American Jewish civil rights volunteers, who participated in numbers disproportionate to their share of the population, understate the Jewishness of their activism, either out of humility or due to subsequent conflicts between parts of the Jewish and African American communities. Iris Geller's story intersects with several of these frameworks, and yet it is unique, adding new perspectives to an ever-expanding literature on the civil rights movement.

Iris Geller was a "good girl," a nice Jewish girl, who was such a true believer that she was willing to uncharacteristically defy her family, leave college for the South, and organize in increasingly challenging situations to fight back against racism, which she considered a perversion of American democracy. Such pugnacious willingness to fight for our democracy is imperative today as the current administration attacks civil rights, women's rights, LGBTQ rights, immigrant rights, and diversity, equity, and inclusion initiatives. As each generation identifies its political priorities, we need to know about regular people who took personal risks to stand up for what is right. Iris Geller is one such person, one you will be delighted to get to know.

In *No One Ever Asked: The Untold Story of A Civil Rights Worker*, the question naturally arises: Why didn't Iris's relatives ask about her activism? Were family members not interested in their relative's seven-year commitment to one of the twentieth century's most generative social movements? So as not to "upset Aunt Eva," younger family members were told not to ask about her daughter Iris. "No one asked" because it was complicated to be a white Jewish woman ally in the southern civil rights movement in the mid- to late 1960s. That involved what my own Jewish grandmother called "rocking the boat"—something middle-class, mid-twentieth-century American Jews were clearly keen to avoid. Yet Iris Geller broke with her family and went south to join the movement for the first time in 1965, a year after the whole world knew that the Klan had killed civil rights workers James Chaney, Michael Schwerner, and Andrew Goodman. In fact, Iris's first civil rights action was to carry a sign bearing the image of Andrew Goodman at the Atlantic City demonstrations outside the 1964 Democratic National Convention. There she heard Fannie Lou Hamer's riveting testimony on the brutal treatment she received for trying to register to vote. When Mrs. Hamer pointedly asked, "Is this America?" Iris Geller was among those idealistic young people moved to grapple with the question by getting involved.

Rochvarg weaves a gripping narrative that draws the reader into Iris Geller's evolving commitment. While well grounded in contemporary civil rights scholarship, the story is written with an engaging warmth and dry wit. Hints of a biracial child at the book's beginning grab the reader and signal Iris Geller's willingness to transgress her era's race and gender norms.

Now a retired University of Baltimore law professor, Rochvarg served as a young lawyer for one of the Watergate defendants. It is moving that a witness to such an epic tale of political hubris actively pursued his cousin's modest but no less significant story. That impulse resonates with a second wave of civil rights historiography eschewing a focus on charismatic male leaders. Initiated by historian John Dittmer in his now classic 1994 book *Local People: The Struggle for Civil Rights in Mississippi* (University of Illinois Press), this scholarship centers local southern people—particularly grassroots African American women and the young organizers who learned from them—as the backbone of the civil rights struggle. It also adds to a growing literature of personal narratives by black and white movement women, including the exemplary *Hands on the Freedom Plow: Personal Accounts by Women in SNCC* (University of Illinois Press, 2010).

Iris Geller's story makes several additional contributions. It highlights one woman's process of political awakening, the journey of a white ally whose commitment was not performative but genuine. We need to understand what moves ordinary citizens to act in pursuit of justice. For Iris, that moment came as she watched TV footage of Selma's Bloody Sunday. Soon after, she responded to a campus poster recruiting volunteers for a southern voter registration project. Led by Dr. King's Southern Christian Leadership Conference (SCLC), she joined SCOPE, the Summer Community Organization and Political Education project.

Iris's experience helps to expand the triumphalist 1954–65 civil rights narrative (from *Brown* v. *Board of Education* to the Voting Rights Act) by focusing attention on post-1965 challenges. These included resistance to school integration and to implementing the Voting Rights Act. SCOPE also linked voter registration to poverty, a focus Dr. Martin Luther King Jr. would articulate most explicitly by launching the 1968 Poor People's Campaign right before his assassination.

As a new volunteer at SCLC's orientation, Iris was thrilled to hear such luminaries as Dr. King and his SCLC colleagues Ralph Abernathy, Hosea Williams, and James Bevel; historians John Hope Franklin and C. Vann Woodward; long-time activist Bayard Rustin; civil rights attorney Joseph Rauh; nonviolent direct action mentor James Lawson;

and future UN ambassador Andrew Young, among others. However, the most valuable parts of her in-depth SCLC story deromanticize the everyday struggles, tensions, and tedium of movement work. She learns how to deal with physical and cultural differences in staying with her host family in the Black community. As she faces isolation, sexism, mundane tasks, frustration at modest outcomes, and disappointment in one of her heroes, Iris matures, and her commitment grows.

A call for reinforcements in the racially heated town of Americus, Georgia, brings Iris into greater contact with African American women leaders, radical SNCC activists like John Lewis, mass marches, all-night vigils, Klan marches and killings, and federal intervention. Detailed chapters on SNCC work in Columbia and Greenville, two less visible Mississippi communities, add new dimensions to understanding the post-1965 era. The Greenville chapter illuminates grassroots, coalitional, antipoverty work, including an audacious occupation of the Greenville Air Force Base. The stakes grow higher.

When Iris returns home from the South for the first time, even complete rejection by her parents does not stop her. She moves out and begins to shape her own life. Like the young women I wrote about in *Going South: Jewish Women in the Civil Rights Movement* (New York University Press), Iris Geller came of age during the time of *The Feminine Mystique*. That was a time when middle-class white women were expected to go to college, but primarily to find a suitable husband. Watching Iris claim her own agency as an activist is a thrilling repudiation of that mixed message.

Iris Geller's experience also illuminates a controversial but meaningful aspect of some White women's experiences in the movement—defying taboos and demonstrating one's antiracism through intimate relationships. Such relationships were a big risk, given lynching's ugly history (predicated on false accusations of Black men sexually assaulting white women), and the actual danger of the Klan seeing Black men and white women together. Klan members killed Viola Liuzzo, a white mother and volunteer who was driving a young African American man home after the 1965 Selma to Montgomery march. It is also complicated to analyze interracial movement relationships because some movement veterans and scholars have felt that early feminist theorists overstated movement men's sexual exploitation of white women activists. Nonetheless, several of the women I interviewed cherished those relationships while recognizing their complexity.

The tender and understated story of Iris Geller's relationship with Curtis Styles, a veteran SNCC activist from Mississippi, provides a nonsensationalized opportunity to understand how such relationships evolved. Styles introduced Iris to SNCC's history, grassroots organizing methods, egalitarian vision, legendary fearlessness, and radical mystique. Iris only becomes more audacious when she quits college to join SNCC in Mississippi.

Styles also tells Iris about the numerous Jewish women volunteers in the 1964 Mississippi Freedom Summer Project. He introduces her to Ira Grupper, one of the SNCC veterans to most consistently probe the relationship between Jewish identity and antiracist activism. Grupper, who died recently, sought to help Iris heal her broken relationship with her mother, positing himself as a nice Jewish boy from Brooklyn who would look out for her daughter. Themes of Jewishness appear regularly throughout the narrative, offering fertile ground for further analysis. These include immigrant origins, moving into the middle class, shame, silences, and the family's shunning of Iris as part of the American Jewish assimilation project. The heartwarming, seemingly contradictory story of Eva Geller's secret communication with her defiant daughter Iris evokes themes of fierce protectiveness and ambivalent pride. For further exploration, see historian Joyce Antler's book, *You Never Call!, You Never Write!: A History of the Jewish Mother* (Oxford University Press).

Stories of earnest young women like Iris abound in the postliberal cities of the North, providing much-needed models of how to serve as antiracist allies. White volunteers had to undergo a rigorous application process to take part in civil rights projects. Those who made the cut teach us what it looks like to submerge your own ego, follow Black leadership, and be willing to put your life on the line for a cause not immediately your own. This is particularly important at a time when the gains of the civil rights movement are under direct attack. A May 2025 executive order mandates that federal agencies cease to use "disparate-impact liability," a core concept used to implement the 1964 Civil Rights Act.

Narratives of people like Iris Geller are precious resources in America's ongoing struggle to achieve a true multiracial democracy, the vision that inspired young civil rights workers from many backgrounds to risk their lives under the leadership of grassroots African Americans. If it becomes impossible to protect the laws that civil rights workers fought and died for, we will need inspiration to create new forms of activism appropriate to the present moment. May the memory of Iris Geller and those like her serve as a blessing in this effort.

Dr. Debra Schultz
Historian, author of *Going South: Jewish Women in the Civil Rights Movement*

NO ONE EVER ASKED

INTRODUCTION

MY COUSIN IRIS DISAPPEARED from 1965 to 1972. None of us thought she had been kidnapped and was being held hostage, but no one in the family had any idea where she was or what she was doing. We missed her at one family gathering after another. Moreover, we were not allowed to ask anything about her, for the oft-repeated reason that "we don't want to upset Aunt Eva," Iris's mother. But even after Iris finally reappeared, we still could not ask "Where were you?" or "What were you doing?" Any mention of Iris's disappearance remained totally forbidden.

Nevertheless, various rumors about Iris's whereabouts and activities during the years she had gone missing circulated, none of which were ever confirmed. The most repeated rumor held that she had "joined the civil rights movement." What that entailed, however, no one knew or tried to explore. I never came across her name in all the books I read on the history of the movement. And since her reappearance, she had lived a quiet life as a social worker, wife, and mother of two. But I remember wondering: What was her story? Almost fifty years later, finding myself still wanting to know Cousin Iris's story—if indeed there was much of a story to know—I nervously decided to break the taboo and ask her if she had ever told anyone about what had transpired during that time, and whether she would be willing to do so now. I emailed her, but I worried that I might have intruded into private matters of her life that she had no desire to share with me or anyone else.

My decision to contact Iris about her story stemmed from several factors. When my wife and I got engaged in 1993, she asked about my family members. When it came to Iris, I described her as a married social worker, the mother of a son and a daughter. I added that there was some degree of mystery about her, explaining the little I knew about her seven-year disappearance and adding that upon her return, Iris had introduced to our family a little biracial girl as her daughter. Out of a combination of politeness and perhaps awkwardness, no one questioned Iris about our new family member. A possible opening into the mystery came when, almost thirty years after Iris's reappearance, Aunt Eva died. Now, of course, the admonition "Don't upset Aunt Eva" no longer applied. Still, after so much time had elapsed, maybe it was simply best not to press Iris. In any case, no one did so.

Another reason I finally decided to contact Iris was that many years earlier, as a young lawyer, I was a member of the legal defense team for one of the Watergate defendants, handling the appeal of his conviction for conspiracy to obstruct justice.[1] One of my co-workers and I were by far the youngest people involved in the case. We recognized that at some point in the future, we might well be the last people alive who had any personal experience with the Watergate case, even if we also recognized that our personal roles in it were largely insignificant. Over the years, many people encouraged me to write a book about my experience with Watergate, to tell my story before it was too late.[2] Eventually I did so. And even after the publication of my book, I continued telling others more of what I knew by writing a number of law journal articles about the legal issues involved in the Watergate case.[3] Included in my writing were reflections on having personally participated in such a historically significant case. Almost twenty years after my book was published, I received a telephone call from John Dean, White House Counsel for President Richard Nixon from July 1970 until April 1973 and one of the most famous participants in the Watergate case.[4] He conveyed to me that people involved in historical events have a certain obligation to share their experiences so that others might learn from them—and that this is true even if the stories come from people who do not consider their roles in history to be significant. After this conversation, I thought again about Iris. If she had been involved in the civil rights movement, even only in a marginal way, wouldn't she share that experience? Might she have a story to tell that could teach, inspire, or motivate others? There had been about fifty years of silence since Iris's disappearance. I thought it was time for that silence to end.

In my email to Cousin Iris, I wrote that I had heard that back in the mid-1960s, she had quit college and joined the civil rights movement, and that this had created a rift between her and her parents. I also told her about my own interest in the history of the civil rights movement and asked her whether anyone had ever contacted her about her experiences during that pivotal time in our nation's history. Having received no reply for several weeks, I concluded that she had no desire to talk about this period in her life. This was, after all, consistent with the fact that she had never opened up to our family about her time away from us. A few weeks later, however, I received a response from her. In it, she apologized for not having gotten back to me sooner, then wrote: "You are the first in the entire family to raise the subject of my work during the civil rights movement, and certainly the first to ask questions and express interest. I am quite moved. I am even surprised that you knew that I had participated. This was such a hush-hush issue. I would love to know how you found out."

Her reply left me both relieved and excited: relieved because she had not taken offense at my inquiry; excited because I decided then and there that I would try to write a book about the civil rights movement through the personal experiences of an actual participant in it. I had no idea what I would learn, but Iris agreed to tell me her story. Over the next few years, I met with her and discussed the period of her life that no one had ever asked her about. She remembered many events in detail. Other matters, especially certain names, she could not recall. We agreed to certain rules involving confidentiality as well as which topics and people would remain off-limits. I would follow up our in-person conversations with emails seeking clarification about this or that event or detail. Thus began my research and then writing of a civil rights worker's untold story, one kept a secret for over fifty years.

Many books have been written about the civil rights movement. Most of them tell the stories of the movement's leaders, especially those of Martin Luther King Jr., John Lewis, Stokely Carmichael, and Malcolm X. For every civil rights leader whose life has been the subject of a book, however, there are hundreds, probably thousands, of unknown civil rights workers whose stories have never made print. Now, sixty years after the height of the movement, many of these stories are in danger of being lost forever. Most civil rights workers from the 1960s have died or lost the capacity to share their experiences.

Recent political attempts to erase "uncomfortable" events from the teaching of American history[5] make it even more important today to learn something about those who were so committed to racial, social, political, and economic justice that they upended their own lives and risked their personal safety to bring about change. The issues that motivated these people to get involved in the movement in the 1960s— suppression of voting rights, economic inequality, educational inequality, racial violence, housing inequities, health care disparities, and racism, all of which are part of Iris's untold story—are issues we face today. So many stories of the past should not remain untold. In the pages that follow, I endeavor to tell one of them.

CHAPTER 1

Atlantic City

IRIS IS THE DAUGHTER of Eva and Morris Geller. Eva Geller, born Eva Rochvarg, was the eldest of the five children—three boys and two girls—of Charles and Yetta Rochvarg. Charles and Yetta immigrated to the United States and settled in Philadelphia, Pennsylvania, at the beginning of the twentieth century. They came from the city of Zhytomyr, located about eighty miles west of Kyiv in today's Ukraine. All their children married and remained in Philadelphia; among them they had a total of nine children. I am Charles and Yetta's youngest grandchild; Iris, six years older than me, is the third eldest. Because of our age difference, when we were younger I did not have much interaction with Iris beyond the occasional family gathering. At one such event I noticed Iris's absence. When I asked my father about it, his response was one that would be repeated many times thereafter: "Don't mention Iris. Don't ask anything about her. Don't upset Aunt Eva."

After arriving at Ellis Island from Europe in 1908, Charles and Yetta made their way to South Philadelphia and settled there. In the first half of the twentieth century this neighborhood was home to many Jewish and Italian immigrants; it also had a Black population. After Eva married Morris in 1939, the couple also chose to live in South Philadelphia, not far from Eva's parents. By the time Morris and Eva had Iris in 1946, her parents, grandparents, aunts, uncles, and cousins all lived in South Philadelphia. Iris spent her early childhood years playing and attending school with Jewish, Italian, and Black children in this mixed-race area of the city. In 1952, however, Eva and Morris joined the migration of White residents from South Philadelphia to the northeast section of town. Shortly after World War II, many homes, mostly rowhouses, were built on former farmland north and east of Center City, a new residential area of Philadelphia dubbed the Northeast. Those who left the inner city for the Northeast were overwhelmingly White and heavily Jewish.[1] This, too, typified the student bodies of the section's public schools, including Northeast High School, from which Iris graduated in 1963.[2]

For most of the residents of Northeast Philadelphia, Atlantic City, New Jersey, was the favored vacation destination.[3] Once at the shore, students from Northeast High as well as recent graduates now in college knew where to find their friends—Hi-Hat Joe's on the boardwalk at Chelsea Avenue. Hi-Hat Joe's was a snack shop that served frozen custard, soft drinks, candy, and hot dogs. It was next to a pinball and Skee-Ball arcade. On any given summer night, one could find many Northeast High teenagers hanging out there. For its 1964 national convention, the Democratic National Committee (DNC) decided to convene in Atlantic City. It was a foregone conclusion that the incumbent, Lyndon Baines Johnson, who had ascended to the presidency less than a year earlier after the tragic assassination of President John F. Kennedy, would be the DNC's presidential nominee. Johnson was also heavily favored to win the November election against Barry Goldwater, the Republican Party's nominee, who was generally viewed as too right-wing for mainstream American voters. Except for the uncertainty about who Johnson's vice-presidential running mate would be, no one expected much drama to unfold at the DNC convention[4] to be held at Convention Hall, the annual venue of the popular (at the time) Miss America Pageant.[5] For most of the South Jersey vacationers that summer, the convention was something they had likely heard about, but it interested them only slightly, if at all. None of them could have predicted the controversy and publicity that would surround it.

The 1964 DNC convention was held at the end of August, meaning that Iris would have been about to begin her sophomore year at Temple University in Philadelphia in a few weeks. The family of a girlfriend of hers was renting a place in Atlantic City and had invited Iris to stay with them. This was the week of the convention. On every previous trip to Atlantic City, Iris and her friends would typically spend the day on the Chelsea Avenue beach, walk the boards after dinner, and hang out until about eleven. But this year, Iris had other thoughts. Unlike most of her fellow Northeasters, Iris was excited that the DNC convention was being held in Atlantic City. During the summer she had closely followed the news of two events from Mississippi, a state that hardly anyone from Northeast High cared or even thought about. The two events that had captured Iris's attention were the killing of three civil rights workers in Mississippi a few months earlier, and the dispute within the Democratic Party over who should be seated as Mississippi's voting delegates at the DNC convention. Before this summer, Iris's interest in the civil rights movement had been minimal, but these two events aroused her greater interest.

It was during the summer of 1964, often referred to as Freedom Summer,[6] that three civil rights workers were killed in Philadelphia, Mississippi. These killings drew attention in Northeast Philadelphia for two reasons. First, the obvious one: No one in Philadelphia, Pennsylvania, knew there was another Philadelphia, let alone in Mississippi. Moreover, the murders of the three civil rights workers got special attention in Northeast Philadelphia because two of the victims, Andrew Goodman and Michael Schwerner, were young Jewish men. This created much discussion among the Northeast's large Jewish population, even for those who had never before shown any concern about the civil rights movement.

In late 1963 a coalition of civil rights organizations calling itself COFO—the Council of Federated Organizations—had begun a campaign to increase Black voter registration in Mississippi. For this task it recruited about three hundred volunteers from colleges across the country. Most who volunteered were White and attending northern colleges. A training session was held for the volunteers at Miami University in Oxford, Ohio, where they learned not only about voter registration but also about the dangers involved in doing civil rights work in Mississippi, the deepest of the Deep South states. When told by US Department of Justice (DOJ) officials that the federal government could not offer protection from the violence they might face, some of the students gathered there decided to return home.[7] But most of the student volunteers, even if frightened, did not change their minds, and they traveled to various locations throughout Mississippi to work with local activists. One such volunteer was Andrew Goodman, a student at Queens College in New York. In Mississippi, Goodman was teamed with a local Black activist, James Chaney, and Michael Schwerner, a recent graduate of Cornell University. Both Chaney and Schwerner were working with one of COFO's organizations, the Congress of Racial Equality (CORE), in Meridian, Mississippi. Although their primary focus was voter registration, Chaney, Goodman, and Schwerner were asked by CORE officials to gather some facts about a recent bombing at the Mt. Zion Methodist Church near the town of Philadelphia.[8] Mt. Zion had hosted several civil rights meetings, and there were plans to open a "Freedom School" in the church where local Black residents, both youths and adults, could take classes. On their way to Philadelphia, police pulled over the car in which Chaney, Goodman, and Schwerner were riding and took them into custody. Chaney, the driver, was held on the allegation that he was speeding. Schwerner and Goodman were held as possible suspects in the Mt. Zion Church burning, even though both had been in Ohio at the time. The arresting officer was a Neshoba County deputy sheriff and a member of the racist, terrorist organization the Ku Klux Klan (KKK). The police held Chaney, Goodman, and Schwerner in the county jail in Philadelphia for only a few hours. Upon their release, just after midnight, they were told to get out of town. Not having heard from the three the next day, those back at the CORE headquarters launched a search for them. Already, many feared that they had been killed.

The search for the three men continued for almost two months. Hope they would be found alive dwindled with each passing day. Mississippi newspapers and politicians, however, claimed that the disappearance of the young men was a hoax, one fabricated to create sympathy and support for the civil rights movement. Some maintained that the three missing men were Communists and secretly vacationing in Cuba as guests of Fidel Castro.[9] The media and politicians in other southern states spread similar nonsense. National media coverage of the three men's disappearance was extensive. FBI director J. Edgar Hoover became personally involved in the investigation and assigned many FBI agents to search for dead bodies in Mississippi swamps. Interest and political pressure grew so intense that President Johnson insisted that he be personally briefed on the status of the investigation of the three missing civil rights workers.

While looking for Chaney, Schwerner, and Goodman, searchers found the decomposed bodies of eight Black men. Only three of the corpses were identifiable; they had been civil rights workers. Finally, on

August 4, nearly two full months after their disappearance, searchers found the bodies of Chaney, Goodman, and Schwerner in an earthen ditch. Goodman and Schwerner had been shot at point-blank range. Chaney, the Black man, was shot three times after being beaten. It was subsequently established that shortly after the three men's release from jail, KKK members had ambushed and killed them.

The original goal of Freedom Summer was to increase the number of Black people registered to vote in the South. The program was not successful in significantly registering new Black voters; it was estimated that in 1964, out of 170,000 Black people who tried to register to vote, fewer than 10 percent managed to do so. Sadly, the "success" of Freedom Summer turned out to be the widespread national attention it brought to the dangers that civil rights workers faced when trying to improve the lives of Black people in the South. Some felt, however, that the attention created by the murder of the three young men in Philadelphia, Mississippi, had gained traction only because two of the victims were White. For many years prior to the tragedy, murders of Black people in Mississippi had almost all gone unnoticed and unmentioned. The media coverage of the murders of Chaney, Schwerner, and Goodman, however, caught the attention of many Americans, including my cousin Iris, who thereafter started to follow civil rights stories from Mississippi and other southern states more closely.

The next development relating to the civil rights movement that caught Iris's attention that summer was the planned challenge to the Mississippi delegation to the Democratic Party's national convention by members of the Mississippi Freedom Democratic Party (MFDP). The regular Mississippi Democratic Party (MDP), which had been the dominant political party in Mississippi since Reconstruction, employed a multistep process to select its delegates to the Democratic Party presidential nominating convention in Atlantic City. This process excluded any participation by Black Mississippians; only White people were eligible to vote for and serve as convention delegates. In April 1964, in anticipation of being totally excluded from the delegate selection process, Black activists under the umbrella group COFO, the same coalition of civil rights organizations responsible for the Freedom Summer project, decided to form a new political organization, the Mississippi Freedom Democratic Party, to challenge the all-White convention delegate selection process. Throughout the summer, COFO and the MFDP held precinct and district caucuses around the state. These caucuses were open to both Black and White voters. In early August the MFDP held a convention in Jackson where over two thousand attendees elected sixty-eight people as delegates to the upcoming Atlantic City DNC convention. Of these sixty-eight delegates, twenty were women and sixty-four were Black. One of the Black men, Aaron Henry, was elected chair of the delegation, and a Black woman, Fannie Lou Hamer, was elected vice chair.

The MFDP delegates traveled to Atlantic City with the goal of challenging the seating at the national convention of the all-male, all-White MDP delegation. The MFDP delegates lobbied delegates from other states to urge the Democratic Party's Credentials Committee to reject the MDP delegates and recognize the MFDP delegates as the proper Mississippi delegates at the nominating convention. The committee was scheduled to meet a few days prior to the official opening of the convention to certify delegates from each state. Besides the lobbying by MFDP members in hotel rooms and meeting rooms inside Convention Hall, supporters held demonstrations in favor of the MFDP delegates on the boardwalk.

The night before the convention officially opened, MFDP supporters organized a twenty-four-hour nonstop vigil on the boardwalk in front of Convention Hall, where they held up signs proclaiming that the MFDP delegates were the only legitimate delegates from Mississippi and sang familiar civil rights songs such as "We Shall Overcome." Some of them carried large photographs of Chaney, Goodman, and Schwerner. Some also brandished placards bearing a photograph of the burned station wagon the three men had been riding in when they came under attack by KKK members. At times, MFDP supporters were joined on the boardwalk by MFDP delegates. Delegates from other states that supported the MFDP also joined the marching, chanting, and singing on the boardwalk. The number of people in support of the MFDP was estimated at times to approach four thousand.

Joining this demonstration was Iris, who carried a poster-sized picture of Andrew Goodman as she marched in front of Convention Hall. While marching, she recognized a few people from Northeast High who had gathered to watch the crowd, but she did not know anyone who was demonstrating. Iris marched on the boardwalk with her picture of Goodman until after midnight. The next morning, rather than riding a bicycle on the boardwalk and then going to the beach, as had been her usual routine during Atlantic City vacations, she headed straight back to Convention Hall and rejoined the ongoing demonstration, which had not paused overnight. Hope and a sense of excitement that the demonstrations might convince the Credentials Committee to seat the MFDP delegates seemed to permeate the air. No longer just an observer, Iris for the first time was a participant. To add to the excitement, television crews appeared along with newspaper journalists.

The MFDP supporters set up loudspeakers on the boardwalk to broadcast the Credentials Committee hearing being held inside the convention center. A few people brought small portable black-and-white television sets with rabbit-ear antennas, plugging the sets into electrical outlets on poles. Among those scheduled to speak at the hearing was MFDP vice-chair Fannie Lou Hamer. Everyone was anxious to hear her testimony. Iris heard others talk of their admiration for Hamer and how confident they were that her testimony would win over the Committee. Hamer had compelling stories to share about the treatment of Black people in Mississippi. She had been a victim of an unconsented forced sterilization while hospitalized for an unrelated medical condition. She had been beaten in a Mississippi jail and suffered permanent injuries for engaging in voter rights activities. Moreover, she was a compelling speaker.[10] Her grammar was not always proper, but she was quite engaging and persuasive. The drama surrounding the credentials battle and her planned testimony convinced the television network managers to broadcast her testimony live.

When Hamer got to the microphone at the witness table, the boardwalk demonstrators stopped their marching, chanting, and singing to listen to her testimony over the speakers and watch her on the portable television sets. Hamer's testimony did not disappoint her supporters. She spoke of the racism and violence she had experienced in Mississippi. She recounted the hardships she faced when she tried to register to vote. Her testimony was riveting. Excitedly, Hamer was testifying in person just a few hundred yards from where Iris was standing. Iris, like many others, became emotional hearing Hamer's testimony. This was Iris's first encounter with the personal power of the leaders in the movement.

In the nation's capital, President Johnson sat in the White House also watching Hamer give her testimony on television. What he saw did not please him. The convention was supposed to be all about him and his crowning as the Democratic Party nominee for president. Instead, it suddenly seemed to be all about a Black woman from Mississippi who had experienced racism. Johnson made a quick decision to change the narrative. He ordered his media office to inform the White House press corps that he would be holding a press conference from the briefing room within a few minutes. As the press corps scrambled to prepare for what they thought surely must involve a significant development, Hamer's testimony continued. At the very moment she started talking about the beating she had suffered in a Winona County jail, Johnson began his own broadcast. The radio and television networks cut away from their coverage of Hamer and switched to Johnson. As it turned out, the president had nothing significant to report. He had called the news conference solely to move the attention away from Hamer's testimony. When the television coverage abruptly switched from Hamer to Johnson, the boardwalk demonstrators started yelling, "What's going on here?" "Where's Fannie Lou?" "Shut up, Lyndon," and hissed and booed at the television sets. Only after Hamer had completed her testimony did Johnson end his press conference. Johnson's transparent stunt left the demonstrators on the Boardwalk irate, Iris included. "How could he have done this to Fannie Lou?" they complained. "He's no better than Goldwater." When those inside the convention center at the Credentials Committee hearing learned what had happened, they too were furious at Johnson.

Johnson's attempt to keep Hamer's testimony from overshadowing his upcoming nomination failed. Because the broadcast of her testimony had been cut off in the middle of her appearance, all three major networks at the time, ABC, CBS, and NBC, decided to broadcast Hamer's testimony in its entirety that evening. This led to her testimony being seen and heard in prime time by far more viewers than if her live testimony had not been preempted by Johnson earlier that day. During the full broadcast of Hamer's testimony, Iris, along with many others, continued to march on the Boardwalk. Iris, years later, would proclaim that summer's Atlantic City vacation as her most exciting one ever. She found demonstrating for equal rights far more exciting than hanging out in front of Hi-Hat Joe's. After the prime-time broadcast, MFDP delegates came on the boardwalk and personally thanked individual demonstrators, including Iris, for their support. Iris was moved by the expression of thanks she received from people she viewed as so courageous.

It was clear that Johnson had miscalculated the situation with Hamer and the MFDP. Concerned that the controversy over the seating of the Mississippi delegation at the convention would hurt his campaign, he assigned Senator Hubert Humphrey of Minnesota to meet with several civil rights leaders to try to reach a resolution to the problem of seating the Mississippi convention delegates. Among the leaders with whom Humphrey met were Martin Luther King Jr. and Bayard Rustin of the Southern Christian Leadership Conference (SCLC), and Roy Wilkins of the National Association for the Advancement of Colored People (NAACP). Union leader Walter Reuther of the United Auto Workers also participated. Humphrey put forward a plan whereby the MFDP would be granted two nonvoting, at-large seats at the convention. In addition, it was promised that the 1968 DNC convention would ban all segregated delegations. In return, at the current convention, the entire White Mississippi Democratic Party delegation would be seated if they all pledged to support Johnson over Goldwater in the November general election. Humphrey's role in successfully negotiating this compromise solution sealed the deal for Johnson to choose him as vice presidential running mate on the 1964 Democratic ticket.[11]

As things turned out, the compromise plan failed. First, only three members of the White Mississippi delegation agreed to support Johnson.[12] This was undoubtedly based on the president's support for the 1964 Civil Rights Act, which Goldwater had opposed as a member of the Senate. Secondly, after spirited debate, the MFDP delegates rejected the compromise.[13] As Hamer put it, "We didn't come to Atlantic City for no two seats."[14] With the compromise rejected by both sides, Humphrey's plan had clearly failed to resolve the problem. The result was that at the 1964 DNC nominating convention, the regular all-White Mississippi delegation was seated and granted all of Mississippi's delegate votes. The MFDP delegates were totally shut out.

After they were officially excluded from any participation at the convention, the MFDP delegation left Atlantic City and returned to

Mississippi. Demonstrators, including Iris, continued to show their support for MFDP by protesting on the boardwalk, not ceasing until after Johnson had given his acceptance speech and the convention ended. The MFDP and its supporters were keenly disappointed in President Johnson's failure to support the MFDP delegates. Johnson campaign officials claimed that while the president was sympathetic to the MFDP cause, he worried that the seating of the MFDP delegates and the ouster of the White MDP delegates would cost him votes in southern states. In truth, Johnson totally miscalculated the situation; his concern over losing southern votes was misplaced. In the November general election, Goldwater won 87 percent of the White voters in Mississippi, despite Johnson's nationwide landslide victory over him. Although displeased with Johnson over his treatment of them, the members of the MFDP did not withhold their support for his reelection. They felt that they had no other choice.[15]

Because MFDP's support for Johnson lacked any enthusiasm, however, the group's leaders decided to prioritize its resources away from the presidential election to focus instead on congressional contests. In 1964 very few Black people in Mississippi were eligible to vote. Because of the long-standing disenfranchisement of Black people in their home state, rather than try to run their own candidates for Congress in the regular elections, the MFDP held mock elections for congressional seats.[16] About sixty thousand voters, most of whom were Black, participated in these MFDP elections in five congressional districts.[17] The MFDP certified the winners of these elections as the lawful and proper people entitled to be sworn as members of the upcoming Eighty-Ninth Congress. In January 1965, prior to the swearing in of new representatives in the Eighty-Ninth Congress, the MFDP challenged the seating of the five White men elected to Congress in the five districts in which the MFDP had held its own elections.[18] Relying on section 2 of the Fourteenth Amendment to the US Constitution, the MFDP argued that the five White men had been illegally elected because Black people were denied the right to vote in the contests that had elected them. Because under article 1, section 5 of the US Constitution, the House of Representatives itself has the power to decide whether to seat a member in its own body, the MDFP challenge was presented to the full House of Representatives.

Although the MFDP eventually lost its effort to have its nominees seated in the House of Representatives, the party succeeded in getting almost one-third of the House members to vote in favor of seating the MFDP representatives from five Mississippi congressional districts.[19]

Iris had spent her entire vacation in Atlantic City demonstrating in support of the MFDP delegates outside the DNC convention. As mentioned, she did not spend her time in Atlantic City on the beach or hanging out with friends from Northeast Philadelphia. No, she had a more rewarding experience—trying to make a difference by marching, singing, chanting, and carrying large photographs of civil rights martyrs. After participating in the Atlantic City demonstrations, Iris felt a new purpose in life. She had previously read about the civil rights movement in the newspaper and had watched news of the movement on television, but now she had personally participated in it.

The killing of the three civil rights workers in Philadelphia, Mississippi, led during the summer of 1964 to an increased awareness in Northeast Philadelphia of the serious racial inequities in the South, an awareness amplified by the controversy surrounding the seating of the MFDP delegates and Fannie Lou Hamer's testimony at the Atlantic City DNC convention. These events had created a deep well of sympathy among residents in Northeast Philadelphia for the plight of Black people in the South—and, for that matter, about racial injustice in America in general. Iris was now committed to doing all she could to fight for racial equality. She was certain that her parents, Eva and Morris, would agree that working to guarantee equal rights for Black people was a worthy endeavor for a young American. After all, both parents were lifelong Democrats who idolized Franklin Delano Roosevelt because of his leadership during the Great Depression. Working for those in need of help was an accepted rule in the Geller home, a place where discrimination of any kind was unacceptable. Iris's father, Morris, was a clerk at the main post office in Philadelphia, and a proud member and officer of his local postal workers' union. He had strongly supported the recruitment of Black postal workers into the union. He had even rejected promotions within the Postal Service that would have required him to quit the union. Everyone Iris knew in Northeast Philadelphia had supported John Kennedy in 1960 and considered themselves liberals. She had never heard racial slurs uttered at home or at school. She was certain that her new commitment to the civil rights movement would find support among those with whom she interacted. She looked forward to the upcoming fall semester at Temple University and the opportunities her sophomore year would present for her to build on the activism that she had first experienced in Atlantic City.

CHAPTER 2

Temple University

DURING THE 1960S MANY GRADUATES from Northeast High School went to Temple University. At that time Temple was mostly a commuter college, and most of the students from Northeast Philadelphia who attended it lived at home with their parents for financial reasons. Despite being a commuter student, Iris was determined to participate in on-campus activities that would build on her recent activism in Atlantic City.

Iris sought a campus organization committed to racial justice and the civil rights movement. She attended welcome meetings for several organizations, but one student group set itself apart from the others. This group called itself Conscience. Unlike some of the other student organizations at Temple affiliated with national organizations, such as Students for a Democratic Society (SDS) or Young Democrats, Conscience was created by Temple students for Temple students. Michael Simmons, the group's leader, was an exceptional person with an unmatched commitment to racial and social justice.[1] Simmons grew up in the neighborhood surrounding Temple University in North Philadelphia, a far different neighborhood from Iris's Northeast Philadelphia. North Philadelphia was mostly Black; Northeast Philadelphia was mostly White. North Philadelphia was an older area with abandoned houses. Almost all the houses in Northeast Philadelphia were newly built. The original Northeast High School was in North Philadelphia, but a new high school was opened in 1957 in the Northeast and took the name Northeast High, while the original Northeast High School had its name changed to Thomas Edison

High School.[2] Both high schools were de facto segregated by the city's housing patterns.

Iris attended her first meeting of Conscience in September with about ten other students, both men and women, White and Black. When asked to say a word about herself, Iris mentioned that she had recently demonstrated in Atlantic City in support of the seating of the MFDP delegates. Simmons said that he had also been there. The two of them chuckled at the fact that they had not seen one another on the boardwalk. This initial interaction made Iris feel comfortable as a new member of the group. Over fifty years later, when I spoke in person with Simmons, he remembered Iris, even though Iris had told me that she highly doubted he would have any idea of her. Over the years, Simmons remained involved in many human rights issues and became well known for his activism both in the United States and Europe.[3]

Conscience focused on working with Black youth who lived in the area near Temple. For example, the group held an afterschool tutorial program for schoolchildren in the area. It also organized a free breakfast program. Iris helped with both projects. She also worked on developing a summer youth program that combined academics and athletics. Besides their work in the community, Conscience members held meetings in which they discussed numerous current issues. Most of the discussions involved issues of racism. Agreeing that it was not solely a problem in the South, the group was determined to address racism at Temple. They urged the creation of special recruitment and admission programs at Temple for Black students, especially prospective enrollees from the surrounding area, and agitated for the creation of an African-American studies program. The group criticized Temple's plans for physical expansion into the neighboring community, which would uproot Black residents. Simmons arranged meetings to discuss these and other concerns of the group with university officials. Members also debated the effectiveness of a nonviolent philosophy in addressing the problems of racism. They discussed the sit-ins at lunch counters by college students in Greensboro, North Carolina, and Nashville, Tennessee. Should they just sit there and be beaten, or would it be better if they fought back? What about pacifism in world affairs? Unilateral nuclear disarmament? The military draft? European and American imperialism and colonialism? South Africa, apartheid, boycotts, and divestment? Conscience members engaged in spirited debates about all these issues at their meetings.

This integrated group of earnest young adults also discussed the future of the civil rights movement in the United States. They pondered whether Black control of the movement was a better approach than an integrated leadership approach. If the Black community felt it owed its liberation to White people, would this simply perpetuate a type of racist paternalism just as destructive as overt racism? What was the best way to address the political and economic imbalance between Black and White people? Would expanded voting rights for Black people make a difference? Iris and her fellow group members spent hours discussing these issues, which they found both fascinating and challenging. The Conscience meetings became a salon for ideas that Iris participated in fully.

Due largely to her involvement with Conscience, Iris very much enjoyed the 1964 fall semester at Temple, and she continued her active involvement with the group well into the start of the 1965 spring semester. Then an event occurred that would bring about great change in Iris's life. During spring break, Iris fell ill and found herself bedridden for several days. She spent these days mostly watching television. On Sunday, March 7, she was watching the movie *Judgment at Nuremberg* on ABC when the movie was interrupted by a news report anchored by Frank Reynolds from Selma, Alabama. Earlier that day, Alabama state troopers had attacked civil rights marchers on the Edmund Pettus Bridge, which spanned the Alabama River in a small town in rural Alabama. The bridge had been named after a Confederate general who later served as the Grand Dragon of the Alabama Ku Klux Klan. ABC News broadcast fifteen minutes of video showing Alabama state troopers beating defenseless people who had just started a march in support of civil rights for Black people in Alabama. Even more disturbing was that though the marchers had kneeled to pray as the state troopers advanced toward them, the state and local lawmen beat the peaceful assembly with billy clubs and bull whips and sprayed them with tear gas. Some marchers were trampled by mounted troopers. In the face of the attack, some of the marchers passively stood still; others ran for their lives. Some scooped up small children as they ran back over the bridge. Many were wounded and bleeding, and some lay knocked unconscious. Troopers, following orders from their commander over a bullhorn, chased the fleeing marchers, inflicting more pain and injury than they had dealt out in the initial attack. Iris was horrified by what she was seeing on television, as were most Americans. At this point, she knew very little about the events in Selma that had led to what would become known as Bloody Sunday. In just a few months, however, she would not only have learned much more about those events but be driving in a car and personally speaking with one of the men who had stood on the front line of marchers on the bridge that fateful day.

Iris's horror and outrage over what she had just seen on television caused her to call a friend from Conscience. She told her friend that they needed to do something to support the marchers in Selma and protest the police brutality. Her friend informed Iris that Michael Simmons had already started organizing a march on Saturday from Temple University down Broad Street to Philadelphia City Hall, where a rally would be held. The next day, Iris got out of her sickbed and met with other members of Conscience to help publicize the march and rally in support of the Selma marchers. Simmons was clearly the leader, but Iris and others helped with whatever was needed. When Saturday arrived, more than three thousand people gathered at Broad and Diamond Streets on Temple's campus and began a march to city hall.[4] The marchers sang, chanted, and held signs denouncing police violence and racism. A few of them made speeches, but the main impact was the sheer number of marchers, Black and White, old and young, who showed up in support of those beaten in Selma.

After the Selma attack, Iris grew even more determined to get involved in the civil rights movement. Tutoring neighborhood youths through Conscience was important work, and something she enjoyed, but she wanted to make a greater contribution to the cause of racial justice. An opportunity arose not long after she returned to campus after spring break. On a bulletin board in the student center, she spotted a flyer from the Southern Christian Leadership Conference (SCLC), Martin Luther King's organization. The flyer announced a new program that SCLC was organizing for the summer named SCOPE—Summer Community Organization and Political Education. An envelope below the flyer held brochures that included an application. Iris took a brochure. Perhaps this was the opportunity for which she had hoped.

The brochure explained the program in detail, as well as what its coordinators expected from the participants.[5] It also discussed political disenfranchisement among Black people in southern states. In more than one hundred counties in the South's Black Belt (so-called not because of the race of many of its residents but because of its rich, fertile soil), Black people comprised more than 50 percent of the population but less than 10 percent of the registered voters. Unless all citizens, including Black people, were permitted to participate in the political arena, according to the brochure, there could be "no real solution to the problems of the South."[6] With a Voting Rights Act pending in Congress, which was expected to pass within a few months, there would be "enormous challenges" to its implementation. The main SCOPE activity during the upcoming summer therefore would be to work with local leaders in Black communities to conduct voter registration drives in the South. The brochure also discussed how denial of voting rights led to police brutality, pointing out that in Alabama, "police unloose dogs, shock with electric cattle prods and jail hundreds simply because [Black people] want to register to vote. These police were hired by men who were elected, but [Black people] cannot vote." Southern Black people also suffered from inadequate public education, which related to voting rights as well. "The people who keep [Black people] out of good schools are elected, but [Black people] cannot vote. If all [Black people] in Alabama could vote, we could elect people to the government who could stop police brutality and give everyone equal education and job opportunities. Voting is the answer, but we cannot freely vote." Many of the problems faced by Black people were "the direct result of not having the right to freely vote," the brochure argued:

> We have been told that the reasons [Black people] are poor, uneducated and in bad shape is because we are no good. But the real reasons are White Southerners found ways to keep [Black people] from voting: beatings, murders, and lynchings to frighten; literacy tests which [Black people] could not pass because of educational deprivation. In Georgia, half of adult Blacks had less than four years of formal education. States impose poll taxes that cannot be paid because of no education and no jobs. There are laws that

make any person whose grandfather was a slave ineligible to vote. SCOPE will work to end all these problems through voter registration.[7]

Martin Luther King Jr., head of SCLC, had appointed Hosea Williams to lead SCOPE as its director of voter registration and political education. SCOPE would strive to register forty-nine thousand new Black voters in 120 counties in Georgia, Florida, Alabama, Virginia, South Carolina, and North Carolina. Interestingly, Mississippi was not on the list; the previous year, Freedom Summer had shown that the state was too dangerous a place in which to conduct this type of program. Besides voter registration, SCOPE planned to attack problems of educational deprivation and poverty.

SCLC's plan was for colleges to take the lead in volunteer recruitment through each school's office of student affairs. Each college was encouraged to establish a SCOPE chapter that would meet throughout the school year to train students, using materials provided by SCLC. Each summer, chapter members would volunteer in a Black community in a southern state. SCLC would arrange housing for the college students and find local volunteers to work alongside them, in the hope that the individual chapters would remain involved with the same community each subsequent summer.

SCLC provided advice on recruiting volunteers for SCOPE. It was suggested that a screening committee be formed at each college to review applicants. Each such committee should include a mental health professional and an "experienced freedom fighter."[8] "Everyone who is interested in working can be of help, the SCOPE brochure advised, "so screening committees should not be overly rigorous in their judging of volunteers. Working on civil rights in the South requires dedication, courage, and maturity; however, these qualities can and have been acquired by many seemingly dilettante young college students. Anyone old enough to go to college is old enough to work on voter registration. It will be up to the screening committee to weed out persons who they feel are incorrigible troublemakers, or impossible to work with."[9] To aid recruitment, SCLC recommended advertisements about the summer program on campus radio stations and in student newspapers.[10] SCLC could provide posters, buttons, and films upon request.

After carefully reading the brochure, Iris decided she wanted to participate in SCOPE for the upcoming summer. She asked her friends in Conscience whether they too might be interested, and whether they had heard anything about a SCOPE chapter being organized at Temple. None of them knew anything about SCOPE, and no one had time to volunteer because they needed to earn money during the summer. Iris then went to the Office of Student Affairs (OSA) at Temple and asked if the university had any plans to organize a SCOPE chapter. OSA had heard nothing about SCOPE. Iris was the first person to mention it to them.

Iris was disappointed and disillusioned by the lack of information about and interest in SCOPE at Temple. She wanted to volunteer, but SCOPE was relying on partnerships with colleges, and Temple had no intention of participating. She called a telephone number listed in the brochure, explained her situation, and was glad to hear that for students whose college had no chapter, individual applications would be considered. The representative at SCLC also told Iris that he would send her more information. A few days later an envelope from the SCLC Atlanta office arrived in the mail with information aimed at individual, nonaffiliated prospective applicants. The cover letter stated that all individual applicants had to complete an "exhaustive" application, which a SCLC committee would evaluate.[11] Even if approved, however, "in the event that a SCOPE worker turns out to be a persistent trouble-maker, SCLC will retain the right to disassociate him from the project." The materials also explained that each volunteer had to pay their own travel expenses to an orientation in Atlanta in early June, then to the community location assigned, and then back home. Moreover, each worker would pay $10 per week to their host family for room and board. Applicants with cars were encouraged to bring them for use in the project. Because SCLC hoped that SCOPE would be a continuous summer project, each volunteer was expected to create "accurate and comprehensive records of the summers' work" to assure SCOPE's "long range continuity and success."[12]

The envelope also contained a letter from the Medical Committee for Human Rights (MCHR), which had been organized in 1964 to provide medical care to civil rights workers during Mississippi's Freedom Summer. The letter stated that each SCOPE volunteer was required to get a physical examination from their own physician and return the enclosed health form with the physician's signature. This medical examination was at the applicant's own expense. The letter also urged all applicants to "take care of any existent dental needs before you leave your home area." All expenses for medical or dental care once the SCOPE project began remained the sole responsibility of the applicant.[13]

Also enclosed was a release form discharging SCLC of "any and all claims, demands, actions, causes of action, or suits of any kind or nature whatsoever, and particularly on account of all injuries to persons and property, or both, which may result or arise out of the said participation in connection with the . . . summer project. The undersigned executes this release with full knowledge of the hazards and dangers necessarily involved and incidental to working and participating with the summer project."[14] Applicants were required to sign the form and have it notarized. For applicants under the age of twenty-one, a parent or legal guardian had to cosign the release and consent form.[15]

Finally, the application materials included a "Preparatory Reading List for SCOPE Volunteers." The books on the list were divided into three categories: Required Reading, Strongly Recommended Reading, and Supplementary Reading.[16] All applicants were also told to "familiarize" themselves with federal aid programs such as Job Corps and the Neighborhood Youth Program of the Economic Opportunity Act. Iris carefully reviewed all the materials. Without any hesitation, she decided that she would indeed apply. Here was an opportunity that matched her desire to do meaningful work for racial equality in the United States.

Shortly after receiving the information in the mail from SCLC, but before she had started on her application, Iris received a telephone call from the person with whom she had spoken earlier at SCLC headquarters. He told her that SCLC was sending two representatives, Dana Swan and J. T. Johnson, to Temple to talk to students about SCOPE.[17] Maybe, he mused, they would create interest among other Temple students. Experienced civil rights workers, Swan and Johnson had worked most notably in desegregation efforts in St. Augustine, Florida. Almost a year earlier, in June 1964, they were involved in a well-publicized "wade-in" at a Whites-only public beach, organizing an integrated group of swimmers to go there. Johnson had also been involved in desegregation efforts at a private motel pool in St. Augustine, a protest that gained notoriety when the White motel owner poured dangerous amounts of muriatic acid in the pool to force Black bathers out of it. Additionally, Johnson took part in attempts to have White barbers give haircuts to Black men. SCLC had selected St. Augustine—a totally segregated city at this time—in which to implement some of its desegregation efforts because many White northerners stopped there while driving to and from Miami Beach each year. Obviously, the group hoped to raise awareness and gain support for its desegregation efforts from these northerners, most of whom were likely unaware of the treatment of Black people in northern Florida.[18]

A couple weeks later, Iris attended Swan and Johnson's SCOPE recruitment meeting on Temple's campus. Four other Temple students also attended, all of them Black women. None of the other attendees were members of Conscience, and Iris did not recognize any of them. Swan spoke first, telling the gathering about SCLC and its upcoming SCOPE project. Because Iris had already read the information SCLC sent her, she was familiar with just about everything that Swan discussed. One aspect of Swan's presentation, however, struck her: Swan frankly emphasized the downsides of volunteering. He told the group that he could almost guarantee that the host family's housing would be far inferior to what they were accustomed to—no air conditioning, no indoor bathrooms, unpaved dirt streets, noise from trains, no privacy, people of different sexes sharing one room. The food would also probably not be of the quality and quantity to which they were accustomed. Each student, he stressed, should consider these matters carefully before applying. This was no summer vacation. The host families were not operating restaurants or hotels. Swan then warned that volunteering also involved the risk of violence. SCLC could not guarantee that the student volunteers would not risk beatings and even murder, as witness the recent murders of Chaney, Goodman and Schwerner. The decision to join SCOPE, therefore, was a very personal one, and each student had to make it for themself. "Don't feel bad if you decide not to apply," Swan said. "Discuss this with your parents." He reiterated that a parental consent form was required for anyone under twenty-one years of age (which was the case for all five of the students at the meeting), and read the release form that Iris had already seen: SCLC was not responsible for anything that might happen.[19] After telling them that this was a serious decision, and that no one would begrudge them if they decided not to apply, he said he would leave the room for a few minutes and let the five have a discussion among themselves.

After Swan left the room, Iris spoke first. She told the others that she was going to apply. She wanted to do this. The other four said that they would not. One said she didn't think her parents would sign the consent form, and the others chimed in that they doubted their parents would either. Iris didn't think her parents would have a problem with signing the consent form, she said, explaining that she came from a liberal family and that her dad was a union leader who actively recruited Black people into the union. When the others brought up the dangers involved, Iris said she wasn't worried. She wouldn't let racists stop her from doing what she wanted to do. "What about the horrible housing and food?" one asked. Iris said that she could put up with ten weeks of no air conditioning, and it might not be a bad thing to lose some weight.

When Swan returned to the room, Iris told him that she had decided to apply. The others said they had not yet decided but would get back to him. After the others left, Iris stayed to speak with Swan. He told Iris that to get accepted for the summer program, she would need to hold an official individual interview with him. He was leaving Philadelphia soon to visit colleges in other cities but would return to Philadelphia the following week. If Iris completed her application by then, Swan could interview her upon his return. They went ahead and arranged a time for the official interview for the following week.

Iris went home and filled out the application. She only needed her doctor to complete the medical form and her parents to sign the consent form, but when she told her parents about her meeting with Swan and what she had learned about the SCOPE program, their reaction shocked her: they refused to sign the consent form. They were scared that she would get killed, they said, and brought up Goodman and Schwerner from the previous summer. They thought that Jewish students would be targeted. They could not understand why she wanted to live in a house with a poor Black family in the South. It would probably be filthy, they said; she would hate it. And what about the food? The host family probably ate lots of pork, which Iris had never eaten because her family kept kosher. Iris promised not to eat any pork during her summer in the South, but this hardly swayed her parents' position. Why in the world, they protested, did she want to do this? She told them that she felt strongly about the struggle for equal rights for Black people, and that she wanted to take an active part in the civil rights movement. SCLC was Dr. King's organization, she pointed out, and SCOPE, which SCLC sponsored, was a legitimate project in which many college students participated. Her father asked whether she knew anyone else from Temple University who intended to go. "No," she answered.

"You see," he said, "no one else from Temple is crazy like you. You're the only one willing to risk being killed for people you don't know." The discussion had now turned into a heated argument. Her parents then made Iris an offer that they thought would win her over to their side: If she did not go, they would agree to pay for a nose job for her. That is what she could do during the summer! Iris had asked for a nose job when she was sixteen years old, but she abandoned that plan shortly after her parents flatly said no. Coming now, in this context, the offer made her angry; she viewed it as trivializing her sincere desire to work toward racial equality. At this point, she informed her parents that there was no longer any reason to continue the discussion. As she walked up the stairs to her bedroom, her mother yelled, "If you go, don't bother coming back here. If you go, you're not welcome back."

Iris was shocked by what had just happened. She had never seen her parents this angry. They were quiet people who did not get into arguments with others. She was not a rebellious daughter. She still lived at home. She didn't stay out late at night. She didn't drink alcohol, and definitely never used drugs. Her parents were lifelong liberal Democrats. Her father had recruited Black postal workers into the union. Iris could not understand why her parents had reacted this way.

After thinking about what had just happened, Iris developed a plan. She was determined to join SCOPE. She would complete the application and meet with Dana Swan as planned the next week for her individual interview. She would forge her parents' signatures on the consent form. Swan would not know. No one at SCLC would know. As far as the notarized signature requirement was concerned, there were numerous notaries around Temple's campus. She would take the forged consent form and tell the notary that her parents had signed it, although she did wonder if the notary would attach his seal if her parents had not signed the document in front of him. But there was a notary fee; maybe the notary would not be strict. She would take the medical form to her doctor's office and ask someone there to have the doctor sign it. When she was ill, a few months earlier, she had seen the doctor a few times. She doubted that a new examination would be required, that any fee would be charged, or that the doctor's office would contact her parents regarding the matter.

The next day, Iris put her plan into motion. The doctor's office completed the medical form while she waited, without requiring an examination. There was nothing on the form that disclosed why Iris needed it. Another college student was at the doctor's office at the same time to have a similar form completed to serve as a camp counselor that upcoming summer, so the doctor's staff likely assumed Iris needed the form for the same reason. She then forged her parents' signatures on the consent form and took it to a notary near Temple's campus. She told the notary that she needed the form notarized right away, and that her parents had signed it, but since they both worked, they could not be present. Could the notary still notarize it? Having no problem with Iris's request, he duly notarized the consent form. Iris's plan had worked.[20] She would submit the forms to Swan the next week at her official interview to join SCOPE.

The final part of Iris's plan was to tell her parents that she had decided not to apply. When she came back home the next day after class, she told them that she had concluded that they were right about her joining SCOPE for the summer. It was too dangerous. It would not be much fun living in a house with no air-conditioning. The food would be inedible. She would have no privacy. She wasn't joining SCOPE, and it would be better, anyway, to continue tutoring young Black kids during the summer through the Conscience group at Temple. Her parents were greatly relieved. The matter was over. "Let's forget about last night," they said. "Agreed," said Iris. Only a month remained before SCOPE began, but if Iris told her parents the truth, she might not have a place to live until then. She would stay at home under the pretense that she was not joining SCOPE, and when it was time to leave for orientation, she would tell them she had changed her mind.

The following week, Dana Swan returned to Temple's campus to hold individual interviews. Iris was the only person from Temple who had requested an interview. Looking over all the required forms

Iris had handed over to him, Swan declared that everything seemed in order. He then asked Iris to tell him about her interest in joining SCOPE. Iris spoke of having demonstrated the prior summer at the Democratic Party nominating convention in Atlantic City in support of the MFDP delegates, of her involvement with Conscience, and of the profound effect that watching the Selma attacks on television had on her. Swan then asked Iris a few questions. Had she ever been to the South? No, she had never traveled anywhere except Atlantic City. What about the food she ate? Would that be a problem? Iris said that she had never eaten pork, but did not see that as a problem. What about living in a crowded house with a Black family? Iris responded that she understood what was involved. She wanted to go. Swan told Iris that the final decision on her acceptance would be made by the Atlanta office within a week.

The following week, Iris learned by telephone that she had been accepted for the SCOPE program. She was elated. A few days later, she received a letter instructing her to report on June 13 to the SCOPE orientation in Atlanta, Georgia. Orientation would begin on June 14 at 8:00 a.m. She would be staying at Spelman College, a HBCU (historically Black college or university) for women. The orientation programs would be held at nearby Morris Brown College, a HBCU for men with a "brother-sister" relationship with Spelman. The letter went on to say that women were expected to wear long skirts or dresses.[21] No shorts or short skirts allowed. All blouses were to be "modest." Participants should wear comfortable shoes—no high heels. Makeup was discouraged, though not prohibited. Every worker should limit themselves to traveling with only one small suitcase. Clothes could be washed at the host family's home. The acceptance letter did not mention where Iris would be assigned after orientation, or any sort of work schedule for the ten-week summer program.

For the rest of the spring semester, Iris continued to live at her parents' home. When they asked about her plans for the summer, she told them that she would be tutoring students through Conscience. After completing her final exams, Iris spent her days at the Temple University library, reading some of the books on the list previously sent by SCLC. She secretly packed a small suitcase with the clothes she needed for the summer, and withdrew $300 cash from her savings account.

Iris was successful in keeping her plans secret from everyone, most importantly her parents. On June 12, she finally let her parents know of her true plans: She had been accepted into SCOPE and was leaving soon for orientation. They were furious, but Iris said they could not stop her from going. She had her own money and had already purchased a ticket on an overnight bus to Atlanta that would arrive on the morning of June 13. As she walked out the door with her suitcase, the last words Iris heard from her parents were, as promised, "Don't bother coming back."

CHAPTER 3

Atlanta

IRIS ARRIVED AT THE ATLANTA bus station about 8:00 a.m. on June 13 on the overnight bus from Philadelphia. She took public transportation to Spelman's campus, where she located the SCOPE registration desk. She received a name tag, her room assignment in a Spelman dormitory, and a binder with reading materials and the orientation schedule. She looked to find where she would work after orientation, but neither the orientation materials nor the bulletin board at registration bore any such details. She went to her dormitory room and got some sleep. That afternoon she walked over to Morris Brown College, where the male volunteers were staying. She saw other college students who she assumed were SCOPE volunteers, but she did not engage with anyone. That night, dinner was provided at Morris Brown. Iris looked around to see if she recognized anyone. She did not. Most of the others sat with groups of friends from the same college. Students from campus chapters comprised most of the volunteers. Unaffiliated volunteers like Iris made up a small minority. The overwhelming majority of the student volunteers were White, with only slightly more females than males. Although SCLC had an initial goal of about two thousand volunteers, about six hundred college students actually participated. In addition, a hundred and fifty SCLC workers and about four hundred local residents worked with the volunteer students.

After dinner, everyone gathered in the Joe Louis Gymnasium on the Morris Brown College campus. Hosea Williams, the director overseeing SCOPE, welcomed everyone before introducing several SCLC workers. One speaker commented to the group, in a half joking, half-serious manner, to be careful around Williams: "He doesn't stand for any nonsense."[1] The group was then led in song by SCLC workers. The lyrics of the songs were included in the materials that everyone had received at registration. Among the songs they sang together that night were "Ain't Gonna Let Nobody Turn Me Around," "Which Side Are You On?" "This Little Light of Mine," "Paul and Silas," "Freedom," "I Love Everybody," "We Shall Not Be Moved," "Will You Tell It To The Man," "We Are Soldiers," and, of course, "We Shall Overcome."[2] Singing these songs was a staple of orientation. By the end of the week, the volunteers had sung them so many times that all of them had memorized the lyrics. Everyone, including Iris, enjoyed the singing. Once the evening's program ended, Iris returned to her Spelman dormitory room. She had no roommate, although there was another bed in the room. Though she heard chatter from other rooms down the hall, she stayed in her room by herself, wondering what the next ten weeks would bring.

The orientation schedule was packed with programs every day from 8:00 a.m. to 10:00 p.m. Iris attended every orientation session, something many of the other students failed to do. Some of them never even arrived in Atlanta for orientation. Some arrived later that week in the middle of orientation. Still others, although in Atlanta the full week, missed programs because they overslept in the morning or skipped sessions out of boredom or information overload.

Perhaps the busy orientation program had been too ambitious. It was a week-long crash course on numerous topics presented from different perspectives. Programs featured multiple speakers on subjects such as voter registration, living conditions in the South, political organization, nonviolence, self-discipline, and self-protection. Some of the programs offered practical advice. Others provided historical context. Some were more inspirational than informational. Its roster of participants included many of the most famous leaders and intellectuals of the civil rights movement of the 1960s.[3] A short description of each program and its speakers hopefully can provide some indication of the high quality of the SCOPE orientation program and the vast amount of preparation by SCLC officials that was required to present the orientation. The discussion that follows may also demonstrate how tedious and difficult even the most gung-ho college students, those eager to engage in street-level voter registration, found spending hour after hour listening to speeches, even from exceptional leaders.

The first speaker on Monday was Rev. Ralph Abernathy. Abernathy had worked with Dr. King since the Montgomery, Alabama, bus boycott in 1955–56. The Montgomery bus boycott began in response to Rosa Park's arrest for refusing to surrender her seat on a public bus to a White rider. Years later, after King's tragic murder, Abernathy would assume leadership of SCLC. At the SCOPE orientation, Abernathy provided a history of SCLC. It had been operating since its founding in 1957, mostly by members of the clergy. Besides the Montgomery bus boycott, SCLC was instrumental in the 1963 March on Washington, the voter registration drive in Selma, Alabama, and the march from Selma to Montgomery.

Hosea Williams, the leader of the SCOPE project, spoke next. He told the volunteers that SCLC had identified about sixty counties in Alabama, Florida, Georgia, North Carolina, South Carolina, and Virginia where Black people constituted a majority of the population but were woefully underrepresented on the voting rolls. The leaders of SCLC believed that if enabled to vote, Black people in these places might run for and win elections to local offices. SCLC had arranged with local leaders in these counties to work with SCOPE to increase the Black vote. SCOPE also hoped to put pressure on Congress to pass the Voting Rights Act (VRA), legislation that had been pending before Congress for months. When SCLC's leaders first envisioned SCOPE, they expected the VRA to pass Congress and be signed into law by President Johnson by the beginning of the summer. Southern senators, however, had held up the proposed legislation. Although not part of the original goals of SCOPE, the volunteers were now expected to participate in street demonstrations demanding the enactment of the VRA. Several times during Williams's presentation, he paused to castigate some members of the audience for not paying attention, talking, or sleeping. He admitted he was being "tough on people," but this was serious business, and anyone could leave at any time. Before leaving the stage, Williams led the group in several songs, concluding with "We Shall Overcome."

The next speakers were two Black tenant farmers from Alabama who offered practical aspects of voter registration. Many of the people who SCOPE volunteers would be trying to register were illiterate. In Georgia, for example, about one half of the Black population had less than four years of formal education. These people would need help in filling out forms. "Do not assume that the applicant understands the forms that need to be completed. Walk them through each form. Use simple language, but don't talk down to them." The volunteers were told that some potential registrants would express concern that were they to register, they would lose their job. The SCOPE workers were told that they should not promise to protect these people from repercussions from registering. This, after all, was the reality in the South. Several students were selected to do role-playing exercises on getting people to register. This session also ended with songs.

Next to address the students was Bayard Rustin, a very well-known civil rights activist who had worked since the 1940s fighting desegregation, especially in the defense industry. Along with A. Philip Randolph, president of the Brotherhood of Sleeping Car Porters, the first successful labor union led by Black people, Rustin had lobbied presidents Franklin Roosevelt and Harry Truman to end segregation in the armed forces. In 1963 Rustin had organized the March on Washington, where three hundred thousand people heard many speakers, including John Lewis and Martin Luther King Jr. It was at this event that King delivered his famous "I Have a Dream" speech. In 1964 Rustin organized the Freedom Rides to protest segregation in interstate transportation. Rustin recounted the history of the civil rights movement since 1954. He discussed the boycotts, sit-ins, and marches in which he had taken part. He urged the SCOPE volunteers to avoid projecting any sense of superiority. He stressed his belief in the importance of nonviolence to the success of the civil rights movement.[4]

The famous historian John Hope Franklin spoke next. Franklin had worked with Thurgood Marshall and Charles Houston on the NAACP Legal Defense Fund team in developing arguments in *Brown v. Board of Education*,[5] in which the US Supreme Court in 1954 struck down the "separate but equal" doctrine and ordered the end of legally imposed segregated public schools. Franklin's speech was on the topic of myths in the history of Reconstruction. The history of the Reconstruction period had been distorted to glorify what southern Whites called the "Lost Cause." This list of distortions included the falsehood that all northerners who moved to southern states were shiftless, opportunistic carpetbaggers. In truth, many northerners who moved to the South after the Civil War were industrialists who helped rebuild the South. Some of them were idealists who hoped to build a new and just society.

During Reconstruction, newly formed racist groups, such as the Ku Klux Klan, routinely victimized Black people, threatening them with acts of violence and carrying out a great many such threats. In the wake of the Civil War, churches and public schools remained completely segregated. A great many Black people, not permitted to own land, had no choice but to work as sharecroppers. Although Franklin acknowledged some gains for Black people during Reconstruction, such as the Civil Rights Act of 1866 and the Thirteenth, Fourteenth, and Fifteenth Amendments to the US Constitution, by the time Congress officially ended the Reconstruction period, less than ten years after the Civil War, Black people were relegated to second-class citizenship and denied anything close to equal rights.[6] Dinner was served after Franklin's talk.

After dinner, Martin Luther King spoke. He gave what has been described as "a typically rousing speech."[7] His talk covered many areas. He told the SCOPE volunteers that college and high school students were essential to the civil rights movement. When discussing voting rights, King rhetorically asked how a state such as Georgia that denied education opportunities to Black people could demand literacy as a condition to vote. He said he was hopeful that the Voting Rights Act, which would eliminate literacy tests, would be enacted shortly, but that Congress, and especially the Senate, was controlled by "reactionary" people. He spoke of the "triumphant" march from Selma to Montgomery. He urged raising the minimum wage to $2 an hour. In his speech, King also called for a negotiated settlement of the Vietnam War through the United Nations, with the Vietcong, North Vietnam, China, and Russia participating in the talks. At the end of his speech, as the crowd applauded loudly, King walked among the SCOPE students, shaking hands and thanking them for their support.[8] Although she tried her best to squeeze through the crowd of King admirers, Iris could not get close enough to shake hands with King.

King was followed by civil rights attorney Joseph Rauh, whose speech summarized sections of the Civil Rights Act of 1964. Copies of the act were distributed to every orientation participant.[9] After Rauh's presentation, Walter E. Fauntroy, the director of the Washington, DC, chapter of SCLC, spoke. Years later, he would serve in the US House of Representatives for ten terms as the District of Columbia's congressional delegate. Fauntroy discussed the problems with implementing the terms of the Civil Rights Act of 1964 since its passage. When he finished, Fauntroy, well-known for having a beautiful singing voice, led the assembly in song. That ended the first full day of orientation. Exhausting, yes, but what an experience! Like most of the volunteers, Iris went back to her dorm room and fell asleep quickly.

The first speaker on Tuesday's docket was James Lawson, a leading theorist and strategist of nonviolent direct action. Lawson conducted workshops on nonviolence and had been a mentor for future civil rights leaders such as John Lewis and Marion Barry when they were students in Nashville. At the SCOPE orientation, Lawson spoke on the meaning and relevance of nonviolence. A panel then commented on Lawson's speech. Among the commenters was Andrew Young, future mayor of Atlanta and US ambassador to the United Nations. In 1965, at the time of the SCOPE orientation, Young served as the executive director of SCLC and close adviser to Dr. King. Like Lawson, Young spoke of nonviolence based on Judeo-Christian theology.

Next, the students broke into groups and attended workshops led by SCLC staff members. Iris first attended a workshop on what to do if arrested. The suggested approach was to remain nonviolent and not resist arrest but to try to get the name of the arresting officer and identify someone at the scene who could act as a witness to your arrest; once in custody, you should request to speak with an attorney. If brought before a judge without an attorney, ask for a postponement to obtain an attorney. Iris also attended a workshop on what to do if you see someone getting beaten by a police officer. The suggested action was for a group of people to put their bodies between the attacker and the victim, but remain nonviolent: Never attack a police officer. One of the workshop leaders told the students: "Don't bother trying to reason with the police. They don't respond to reason." Among the presenters at this workshop were ACLU attorney Charles Morgan and lawyers who worked for the NAACP Legal Defense Fund.[10]

Following the workshops, the entire group reconvened in the auditorium to hear from James Bevel, director of direct action for SCLC. He spoke on nonviolence and self-defense. Much of his talk was based on the teachings of Mahatma Gandhi. Following a break for lunch, C. Vann Woodward, a well-known professor of American history at Yale University, spoke on the relationship of southern history to the Negro revolution. He encouraged a biracial approach to civil rights activism.

A session on farm labor in the South followed. There, an official from the US Department of Agriculture spoke on issues involving government loans and local farm boards. The day ended with singing.

After two days packed with speeches and workshops by amazing people, most of the SCOPE students began to feel overwhelmed by the amount of information presented. Moreover, only some of the programs seemed relevant to what they expected to do as workers in the field for the SCOPE program. Although they found the historical and philosophical perspectives interesting, the volunteers were not looking for a summer school experience. They wanted action. All were anxious to get to their field locations and start registering people. Still, orientation was less than half over.

Michael Harrington, the author of *The Other America*, a best-selling book that discussed poverty in the United States, started the program on Wednesday. His book, assigned reading in sociology courses at many colleges, was familiar to many of the college students assembled. Iris, for one, had read it at Temple University. Harrington made several points. First, he said that the recent presidential contest between Barry Goldwater and Lyndon Johnson showed that the Republican Party had aligned with southern racists while the Democratic Party had aligned with Black people and the labor movement. Next, he emphasized the importance of job training to end poverty. He also predicted that automation would reduce the need for lower-skilled jobs, something that would have a disproportionately negative impact on Black people. He also criticized the federal Job Corps program for refusing to accept anyone with a criminal record. This, too, disproportionately hurt Black people. Harrington was followed by Vernon Jordan, field director for the NAACP and director of the Southern Regional Council for the Voter Education Project. Jordan spoke on several of the War on Poverty programs recently enacted as part of Johnson's Great Society program. Later in his career, Jordan became well known as a close friend of President Bill Clinton and as a Washington, DC, power broker.

The remainder of the programs on Wednesday covered practical issues relating to voter registration. A panel of people with experience in grassroots voter registration campaigns in the South offered numerous pieces of advice. This panel included Hosea Williams and Randolph Blackwell, field director with the SCLC Voter Education

Project in Atlanta. Iris jotted down in a notepad some of the advice given: "SCOPE workers should organize one or two blocks at a time. Try to develop personal relationships with individual residents, especially local ministers. Find out the reasons why people have not registered to vote. Do not get into any arguments over why they have not registered. Do not compare SCLC to other civil rights organizations with which the residents may have interacted. Never confront anyone in the White community. Spend time talking with young people even though they are under the required age to vote. They can be influential with their parents and other adults. Also, they are future voters. Teach and sing civil rights songs to everyone in the community. Organize community meetings. Even if at first only a few people show up at these meetings, continue to hold the meetings regularly. Tuesday and Thursday nights are usually the best nights for meetings. Find out when church choir practice is held. Avoid any meetings on those nights. Meetings should last about forty-five minutes. Don't let them go any longer. To achieve a successful voter registration drive, each volunteer should be thoroughly familiar with the residency requirements, literacy tests, civics test questions, and the time and place for voter registration. Hold a contest among churches for the largest number of new registrants and the highest percentage of registrants." The SCOPE students enjoyed this practical panel discussion. That night, Iris for the first time felt that the orientation had been useful to what she hoped to accomplish that summer.

Thursday began with several people who spoke on the labor movement in the South. Because of her father's involvement in the postal workers' union, Iris was keenly interested in this presentation, although many of the other students found it boring. The director of the civil rights department of the AFL-CIO, Donald Slaiman, spoke of the need for civil rights organizations and unions to work together. The same southern politicians who were against equal rights for Black people also fought union organization. Next, Leroy Clark, an attorney with the NAACP Legal Defense Fund, discussed Title VII protections for engaging in civil rights activity. For example, any company with more than one hundred employees was prohibited from firing someone in retaliation for participation in civil rights activity. The rest of Thursday was dedicated to discussion of the details of the Voting Rights Act. The

VRA had not yet been enacted, but it was anticipated that it would become law shortly. Speakers included Andrew Young of SCLC and Clarence Mitchell, a lobbyist for the NAACP. Both had worked on the proposed VRA legislation. As usual, the day ended with songs. At the conclusion of the Thursday sessions, the consensus among the students, including Iris, was that the orientation was lasting too long. Everyone was anxious to leave Atlanta and get to work in the local communities.

Friday's session opened with a session titled "Problems of Understanding: North, South, Black, and White." Several speakers spoke about the Black experience in the South. Iris again jotted down some notes. Before the Great Migration from the South to the North beginning in the early twentieth century, 90 percent of the Blacks in the United States lived in the South. Now that number stood at 50 percent. The old trope that Blacks who moved north do so to get on welfare was false and malicious. The mentality of southerners on racial issues would be difficult to change. Almost 70 percent of southern Whites believed that Blacks have loose sexual morals. About 60 percent of southern Whites said that Blacks have dirty homes. About half of southern Whites believed Blacks to be less intelligent, and over one-third of southern Whites thought Blacks are overall inferior to Whites. Many southern Whites did not even recognize Blacks as human beings. Any hope of changing southern White attitudes toward Blacks could only come through social contact. The integration of the military had been a big step in the right direction to changing the perception of Blacks by Whites.

Friday afternoon's session featured Jack Greenberg, director of the NAACP Legal Defense and Education Fund. He warned that local police officers in southern states had no qualms about testifying falsely in court. Most of the cases involving arrests of civil rights workers were heard by local judges in county courts. Volunteers should not expect fairness or justice. SCOPE had arranged for lawyers to be available to anyone arrested. "Until a SCOPE affiliated lawyer meets with you, do not say anything," Iris wrote. "Do not argue with the judge or arresting officer. Do not curse at them. Try to stay calm until the SCOPE lawyer shows up." Iris hoped that what she had just heard would not prove relevant to her SCOPE experience, but she, like the others, understood the potential dangers. She had never spoken with or even met an attorney, but she was glad to know that if she needed one, SCOPE would provide one for her.

Friday night featured a special session for only the women volunteers on the topic of sexuality and the South. (No such program was held for the men.) The women learned that they were not allowed to drink any alcohol while living in their host communities. Getting drunk would reflect very poorly on them as individuals and on SCOPE. They should always wear "proper" clothes, which meant a long skirt with a blouse that was not "low cut," or a long dress with a high neckline. No shorts, no tank tops, and no bathing suits, no matter how hot the weather.[11] Next followed a discussion of interracial dating. This was not allowed, period. A Black man holding hands with a White woman in public in the South would most likely lead to acts of violence against both hand holders.[12] The group was reminded of Emmett Till, the teenager from Chicago who was brutally murdered in Mississippi in 1955 after having been accused of either whistling at a White woman or making a suggestive comment to her.[13] Not surprisingly, many years later, it was divulged that the accusations were false. Additionally, Black volunteers in every local community who had been recruited by the SCLC to help with the SCOPE program had been warned to stay away from White female SCOPE workers. "Stories" had circulated that the White women volunteers were flattered by the attention they received from local Black men. Some of the women might be "curious" about being with a Black man. Some would find the "taboo" exciting. Others might think that having sex with a Black man would prove they were not racist. Regardless of the reason, SCOPE workers should not be involved in any interracial sexual activity. Failure to follow this rule would lead to the SCOPE worker being told to leave the program. To further emphasize the prohibition on sexual relations, a medical doctor spoke of the high rate of venereal disease in the South. The message to the SCOPE women could not have been any clearer. To what extent these warnings were ignored will never be known, but to Iris, they were unnecessary. She had joined SCOPE to work for racial equality and justice. Sexual escapades did not appear on her list of reasons for volunteering.

On Saturday, the last day of orientation, Iris found herself quite anxious to have the orientation end. It had covered too much. Although the speakers were excellent, no one could have absorbed all the information presented. Going from 8:00 a.m. to 10:00 p.m. each day had been exhausting, and she eagerly wanted to get to work on voter registration in her assigned community. She had joined SCOPE to take action, not to listen passively to speeches.

Before the posting of the location assignments, however, the orientation program had a session about the upcoming fieldwork. In each location, SCLC had arranged for local SCOPE offices in churches, businesses, and private homes.[14] Each location needed at least one car provided by either a SCOPE volunteer or a local resident, with location assignments in part based on car availability. All canvassing for voter registration would be done in teams of at least two people. Teams should stay in their assigned street zone, and everyone must always know where the other teams were working. Each group was expected to submit a weekly report to the SCLC Atlanta office. These reports would be used to determine whether anyone should be transferred to a different location. Just because someone was assigned to one location to begin the summer did not mean that they would remain there through the end of the program.

Finally the announcement came that orientation had ended, and all the student volunteers were about to learn where they would be working. In an adjoining room, several bulletin boards listed the names of each SCOPE volunteer and his or her group, the SCLC leader of that group, and the county in which that team would work. Host families would be assigned once the team arrived in the host county. Along with the others, Iris hurriedly walked to the room and started to read the list of names and assigned locations. Most of the teams comprised between six and ten people. When Iris found her name, she was a little confused. Her team had only two people—herself and someone named Boyd Faust. Their location was listed as Savannah, Georgia, and their leader as Hosea Williams, the head of the entire SCOPE program. Iris did not quite know what to think about her assignment. Why only two? And why was Hosea Williams their leader? Iris decided to remain near the bulletin board, hoping to meet Boyd. When she saw a White male looking at her name, she asked if he was Boyd. "Yes, I'm Boyd. Are you Iris?" A few moments later, a SCLC worker came over to the bulletin board and asked if they were Iris Geller and Boyd Faust. After confirming their identities, Iris and Boyd were told that no one from

Chatham County, where Savannah was located, was available to drive them to Savannah. Instead, they would be staying in Atlanta for a few more days at the SCLC "Freedom House," not far from their present location. None other than Williams would drive them there in about an hour. Although disappointed by the delay in getting to work with voter registration, Iris was excited at the prospect of working closely with Williams.

Iris and Boyd went to their rooms to pack their belongings and met back at the same bulletin board to wait for Williams to drive them to the Freedom House. As they waited, they learned a little bit about each other. Boyd's background was very different from Iris's. He attended University of Notre Dame in Indiana, was Catholic, and had grown up in McComb, Mississippi, a small rural town with a history of serious racial tensions.[15] In 1961, when Boyd was in high school, a local civil rights activist, Herbert Lee, was killed. Over the next several years, Black churches in McComb were firebombed. Black people were intimidated with threats of violence.[16] Boyd and his family pretty much ignored these attacks on Black people. They did not approve of them, but they never got involved in any protests or openly condemned the violence in McComb. It was a bit of a culture shock to Boyd when he moved to Notre Dame. Unlike McComb, the campus was mostly White, and there were no overt racial tensions, let alone racial violence. He joined the Young Christian Students (YCS), a religiously oriented student organization on campus. Although considered progressive, YCS was not involved in any direct action social justice activities.

At the time Boyd attended Notre Dame, Theodore Hesburgh was the president of the university. Father Hesburgh was well known for his strong support of the civil rights movement and was an advocate for federal government programs to help Black people. In 1957, President Eisenhower appointed him as a member of the US Civil Rights Commission. When SCOPE was in its initial stages of organizing, Dr. King sent a letter to the presidents of many universities seeking their assistance in publicizing the summer program. When Hesburgh got the letter, he sent it to the president of YCS, who solicited interest among the membership. In response to the letter, Boyd attended a meeting on Notre Dame's campus with Willie Bolden, an officer of SCLC.[17] Bolden had been personally recruited by Dr. King to join SCLC when they first met in Savannah. As had Dana Swan and J. T. Johnson, who had recruited Iris at Temple University, Bolden had participated in the "wade-ins" in St. Augustine, Florida, to protest segregated beaches and swimming pools.

About twenty Notre Dame students attended the SCOPE recruitment meeting with Bolden. When preliminary applications were handed out, only four of the twenty, including Boyd, completed one. When the full application was due, the other three students had abandoned their possible involvement because their parents objected. Even though they were over the age of twenty-one and did not need parental consent (unlike Iris, who had forged her parents' signature), they did not challenge their parents' admonitions. Only Boyd submitted a completed application. He, too, was over twenty-one when he told his parents about his plans to work for SCOPE, and they, like Iris's parents, had been absolutely against his participation. Based on their firsthand experiences in McComb, they feared that working for SCOPE would get their son killed. Boyd argued with his parents, telling them he was determined to go despite their opposition, which led to his estrangement from his family. During the summer in which Boyd worked with SCOPE, his grandfather died. Boyd did not attend the funeral because he felt he would not be welcome. It would be decades before Boyd returned to a normal relationship with his family.

One of the initial conversations between Iris and Boyd centered on why the two of them were the only ones being sent to Savannah. They came up with several possible explanations. First, although from large universities, they had come without any college mates. Second, Iris and Boyd happened to look very young for their age. Although at twenty-one, Boyd was two years older than Iris, he looked more like a teenager. Both recognized their relative youthfulness compared to the other volunteers at orientation. Perhaps Williams, the one who had made the assignments, was concerned that both Iris and Boyd needed more support and oversight than other volunteers who were older, looked more mature, and were in the company of friends from the same college. Assigned to him, they would be under his watchful eye, at least for the beginning of the summer program.

Iris and Boyd also shared their thoughts on orientation, which, as it turned out, were similar. Because each was the sole representative from their college, they had spoken with few others at orientation and felt largely isolated. They also both expressed disappointment with the substantive parts of orientation, which they found more like a motivational rally than a practical training program. The programs and lectures had been strong on inspiration, sociological theory, history, cultural deprivation, and prejudice, but offered comparatively little on how to participate in a voter registration drive, political education, or community organization. Yes, those topics had been covered, but both Boyd and Iris felt unprepared to properly perform voter registration work in a Black community in the South. At least they'd enjoyed the singing!

It also came out that Iris and Boyd were both disappointed to be assigned to Savannah, which had not been on the list of possible places that SCLC planned to send SCOPE workers. This was due mostly to the voter registration work already done by Williams in that city. Indeed, he had discussed his past work in Savannah during orientation. Now Iris and Boyd feared that they were being sent to a place where not much still needed to be accomplished. They felt slighted. The "real action" seemed to lie in those rural locations not previously targeted for civil rights projects.

Boyd and Iris continued talking as they waited for Williams to show up and drive them over to Freedom House. It did not take long for the gymnasium to empty. Everyone else had already left to travel to their assigned locations. Finally, they saw Williams walking toward them. He asked if they were Iris Geller and Boyd Faust. After they replied yes, he repeated what they had been told earlier. No one was available to drive them to Savannah. Until transportation was arranged, they would be staying at the SCLC Freedom House in Atlanta. He also now told them that things in Savannah were not as well organized as they were in the other locations where SCOPE was sending workers. He assured them, however, that everything would work out fine. He was from Savannah, had worked there for many years, and knew and was known by almost everyone there. Without knowing that Iris and Boyd had shared their concerns over not having received adequate training during orientation, Williams told them not to worry about their upcoming assignment. They would "learn on the job," he said, adding, "That's what I did."

Rather than leaving for the Freedom House immediately, Williams asked if they would mind if he sat down and relaxed for a little while and chatted with them. He was tired from running the orientation and could use a short break. Iris and Boyd were happy to be with Williams, the leader of SCOPE, and told him that they would love to learn more about him. He seemed pleased with their interest in him. He then began to tell them about some of his experiences within the civil rights movement. He had been an "outspoken" civil rights activist in Savannah, beginning in 1960. He'd led marches protesting segregated public facilities and organized mass meetings at churches. By 1961 his work had successfully led to the desegregation of city parks, pools, public transportation, and restaurants in Savannah. In 1963 Williams, along with local leaders, formed the Chatham County Crusade for Voters (CCCV).[18] The CCCV succeeded in organizing a voter registration drive among Black residents of Savannah and surrounding Chatham County, which led to a significant increase in Black voters. Williams repeatedly told Iris and Boyd that the key to success was hard work. Because of his success in Savannah, he had been recruited by Martin Luther King Jr. as a top official with SCLC. Williams then asked if Iris and Boyd wanted to hear about Selma. "Of course," they replied. He then regaled them with his story of Selma, and what might have been his most famous role in the civil rights movement.

At the end of 1964 SCLC set up an office in Selma, Alabama, to help with voter registration of Black people. Another civil rights organization, the Student Nonviolent Coordinating Committee (SNCC, pronounced "snick"), had already been working in the community for several years on civil rights matters, including voter registration, but SCLC felt that voter registration was not moving forward quickly enough. In early January 1965 SCLC held a mass meeting in Selma at which Dr. King spoke to mobilize the voter registration effort. His speech at the mass meeting was attended by about seven hundred Black residents of Selma and the surrounding area. Shortly thereafter, King and John Lewis, the head of SNCC, met and agreed that SCLC and SNCC would work together in Selma. King then dispatched Williams to work along with Lewis to lead the effort to register Black people in Selma. This was no easy task. On January 19 Williams was arrested for his voter registration activities. Fortunately, he was quickly released from custody, and no charges were brought. During his time in Selma, Williams spoke at several mass meetings at the Brown Chapel AME Church, the headquarters for the registration drive.

Williams went on to speak of his involvement with the planned march from Selma to Montgomery. A couple days prior to the event, it was his responsibility to arrange for medical care. Many feared that violence would occur during the march and that injured participants might need immediate help.[19] Williams therefore contacted the Medical Committee for Human Rights (MCHR), which agreed to station nurses and doctors along the route. He also helped work out many of the logistical matters for the march, including arranging food, drinks, and portable toilets.

Williams then discussed what he experienced on the march across the Edmund Pettus Bridge on Bloody Sunday. The original plan was for King and Lewis to start the march to Montgomery together on the bridge, which crossed the Alabama River in downtown Selma. Shortly before the planned day of the march, however, SCLC officials learned that there had been a change in schedule, and King would not be marching in Selma.[20] At this point, Williams met with James Bevel and Andrew Young, two other King aides and SCLC officials, to decide which of the three men would take the SCLC lead position on the bridge in place of King. The two men not chosen for the bridge position would stay in Selma to respond to expected trouble from Alabama law enforcement officials. The decision over who at SCLC would start the march next to John Lewis was ultimately made based on coin tosses. After several coin tosses, Williams "lost"—meaning it was he who was "chosen" to stand beside Lewis.[21]

Come that fateful Sunday, March 7, 1965, Williams took his position on the front line. Facing them from the other direction, only about a hundred feet away, stood a contingent of Alabama State troopers under the direction of Major John Cloud. The troopers were armed and dressed in riot gear. Some of them were mounted on horses. When Cloud ordered the marchers to get off the bridge and turn back into downtown Selma, all the marchers, including Williams and Lewis, following their prearranged plan, knelt in prayer. At that point Cloud shouted, "Troopers advance!" As the troopers charged across the bridge toward them, Lewis and Williams stumbled backward, falling to the ground. Before he could move from where he had fallen, Lewis was beaten with a billy club. Wearing a suit, tie, and trench coat, Lewis lay motionless as more troopers beat him and horses ran over him. Williams, who managed to get to his feet before the troopers got to him, was able to scoop up an eight-year-old girl and carry her to safety through the tear gas, charging horses, and screaming marchers. Once off the bridge, Williams let go of the girl on Broad Street, the town's main street, which led to the bridge. Within a few minutes, everyone was off the bridge. About one hundred of the six hundred marchers required medical care for injuries that included fractured skulls, broken teeth, arms, and legs, bruises and welts from whips, and tear gas irritation. Among the most seriously injured was Lewis, whose skull was fractured. Williams escaped without injury.

After the attack, SCLC and SNCC were even more determined to complete the march from Selma to Montgomery. New plans called for the march to start anew on Tuesday, March 9. On Monday, March 8, Williams, Lewis, and Amelia Boynton filed a class action suit against Alabama governor George Wallace, an outspoken segregationist, Dallas County sheriff James Clark, and other local officials to try to prevent any interference with the planned second march. Williams was the named plaintiff in the litigation, titled *Williams v. Wallace.* The case was assigned to federal district court judge Frank Johnson. Johnson initially refused to make any ruling on the case before a formal hearing was held in his courtroom. Without a court ruling granting an injunction against the State of Alabama and its troopers, the marchers faced the real threat of being attacked again. Wishing to avoid another violent attack, US attorney general Nicholas Katzenbach and President Johnson pressured Dr. King to cancel the march.

Nevertheless, on Monday, March 8, many people had traveled to Selma to support the second march. That night they held a mass meeting to discuss the next day's protest. Most of those assembled were fully prepared to proceed with the march regardless of the pending court case, the wishes of President Johnson, and the very real threat of violence. Before any sort of march commenced on Tuesday, however, Judge Johnson issued an order enjoining the march until he could hear arguments from both sides. President Johnson threatened King that if King did not give orders to cancel the march, he would withdraw his support for the Voting Rights Act, pending in Congress. Among the different civil rights groups and leaders, a split formed over the best course of action.[22] King was concerned about antagonizing President Johnson. He also did not want to violate Judge Johnson's injunction; since the civil rights movement would need to rely on federal court enforcement in future matters, he felt that to flout a court order would be unwise. His position was supported by James Farmer of the Congress of Racial Equality (CORE). On the other hand, SNCC leaders, many of whom were from a younger generation, favored holding the second march notwithstanding the court's injunction.

Behind closed doors, King reached an agreement with Katzenbach. This agreement, however, had not yet been disclosed when about three thousand marchers gathered at Brown Chapel on Tuesday morning expecting to participate in the second march to Montgomery. King addressed the crowd at the church, stressing the need to remain nonviolent: "If you can't be nonviolent, don't get in here. If you can't accept blows without retaliating, don't get in line."[23] After King spoke, those who had assembled at the church marched toward the Edmund Pettus Bridge, singing civil rights songs as they went. They did not know that the script had already been written for what would now transpire.

At the foot of the bridge on the downtown Selma side, a federal marshal stopped the marchers. After doing so, he read the order from Judge Johnson enjoining the march. Rather than turning back to the church, however, the marchers peacefully walked past the marshal and continued to the crest of the bridge. On the front line of the marchers were Dr. King, Ralph Abernathy, the Methodist bishop John Wesley Lord, Presbyterian minister George MacPherson Docherty, and Rabbi Richard Hirsch. From the crest of the bridge, they could see about five hundred Alabama State troopers assembled. The state trooper in command, the same Major Cloud, ordered the marchers to stop. King, Abernathy, Lord, MacPherson, and Hirsch all stopped in place, knelt, and began praying. Major Cloud then gave another order: "Troopers, withdraw." The troopers immediately turned and marched away from the bridge. King then turned to the marchers behind him and shouted, "We'll go back to the church now." Most of the marchers, dumbfounded by what was happening, nevertheless made a U-turn and followed King back to the church. Once there, the marchers learned that he had agreed beforehand with Katzenbach not to violate the court order and to avoid any risk of violence. Although many present were relieved to have avoided a confrontation, many others felt betrayed.[24] SNCC members were especially angry with King over what happened that day, which became known as "Turnaround Tuesday."

The next day, courtroom proceedings began in *Williams v. Wallace*. The hearings took five days. After they concluded, Judge Johnson signed a detailed order lifting his earlier injunction against the march. The order required Governor Wallace and the State of Alabama to "facilitate and protect" marchers from Selma to Montgomery, and for the federal government to assist in this protection. The number of marchers was limited to three hundred when the participants walked along the two-lane stretches of Highway 80. On the four-lane portions of the highway, no limit was placed on the number of marchers. Sunday, March 21, was set as the date the march could begin.[25]

After achieving success in the lawsuit bearing his name as plaintiff, Williams, along with Ivanhoe Donaldson of SNCC, were named coleaders of the upcoming march. Williams and Donaldson would select the three hundred people who would be permitted to march the entire route from Selma to Montgomery. They also helped to figure out the many remaining logistical items. The fifty-four-mile march was estimated to take two full days. Plans had to be made for the provision of food, water, portable toilets, tents, sleeping bags, rain gear, and trash and garbage disposal. Funds needed to be raised to pay for all these things. Security along the route to protect the marchers from expected harassment and possible attacks had to be arranged. Finally, press relations had to be outlined and managed. And all these pressing matters needed to be completed in just a few days. Through the hard work of many, particularly that of Williams, the march from Selma to Montgomery to support voting rights and other civil rights began as scheduled on March 21.

To hear all this personally from Hosea Williams amazed Iris. She had volunteered for SCOPE in great part because of what she had seen on television as she lay in bed ill on Bloody Sunday. Now she had just heard the Selma story directly from one of its heroes. In short, she was in awe of Williams. She found it incredible that she was so physically close to him. For his part, Boyd felt the same way. It was then that

Iris and Boyd had a change of heart about being assigned to Williams as their team leader in Savannah. They were no longer disappointed. After all, no other SCOPE volunteers were working alongside such an important person.

After Williams finished his story about his involvement in Selma, he said he was ready to drive Iris and Boyd to the Freedom House on Johnson Street. It was a short drive. The Freedom House was arranged like a college dormitory, with bedrooms for men and women on different sides of the building and one single-sex bathroom down the hall on each side. Once Iris and Boyd went to their rooms, both of which contained several single beds, Williams told them that he would return when he had more information about their travel plans to Savannah. Iris and Boyd were beyond excited about being with Williams and could not wait to start helping people register to vote. They would finally be working in earnest for the civil rights movement!

The next day, Sunday, Iris and Boyd hung around the Freedom House not really doing much of anything except waiting to go to Savannah. As day turned into night, there was no news from Williams or anyone else. Years later, neither could recall anyone else staying at the Freedom House that day. On Monday, when Williams arrived, Iris and Boyd assumed they would now be on their way to Savannah, but Williams told them that they would not be leaving Atlanta until later that week. He then asked Iris if she wanted to get to work. Iris, thinking that he meant on voter registration, replied yes, she was anxious to get working. Williams said he had work for her—cleaning the bathrooms. He then brought her a toilet bowl brush, toilet bowl cleaner, sponges, and bathroom cleaners and told her to "get to work." Following Williams's instructions, Iris went to the several bathrooms in the house and scrubbed the toilets, sinks, tubs, showers, and floors. About an hour after she had finished, Williams came to her and said, "I thought I told you to clean the bathrooms." When Iris responded that she had, he told her they were not clean enough. She had to clean them all again. Once again, Iris did as she was told.[26] After inspecting the bathrooms a second time, Williams told Iris that her work for the day was over. He did not thank her or comment on her cleaning. He did say that he was going back to his home for the night, and that he would be coming by sometime during the week when he had more information about the trip to Savannah. After Williams left the Freedom

House, Iris recounted her recent experience with Williams and the bathrooms to a few other SCLC workers who were now staying at the Freedom House. She told them that she was upset, but the others replied that Williams's reaction had nothing to do with her. They explained that Williams had a bad attitude toward White northerners. Even with Black volunteers, he was short-tempered, arrogant, and not nice, they said. No one liked him. This came as a surprise to Iris. Only a couple days earlier, she had been so impressed with the man.

Iris and Boyd were very eager to get to Savannah, but they were to spend two more days doing nothing much at all at the Freedom House. Thoroughly frustrated, they considered leaving the program and going back home, but neither was willing to admit to their parents that they might have been right about joining SCOPE. Finally, on Friday, Iris recognized Dana Swan at the Freedom House. As mentioned, it was Swan who had spoken to Iris at Temple University about SCOPE. Swan informed Iris and Boyd that he had been instructed by Williams to drive them to Savannah. Finally welcome news!

CHAPTER 4

Savannah

ON THE DRIVE FROM ATLANTA, Swan explained how SCOPE would operate in Savannah. J. T. Johnson, who Iris had met at Temple, was the director of the Savannah SCOPE project. An office location in downtown Savannah had been secured, but it was not yet operational. Swan told Iris and Boyd that ten other SCOPE workers, none of whom had been able to attend orientation, would arrive in Savannah within the next couple weeks. Some of them would only stay for a short time, perhaps only a couple of weeks. Host families had been found for everyone, but the host families' homes were spread out around the city and its outskirts; therefore, the student volunteers would not be near each other. Boyd would be staying at a home not far from downtown, while Iris would stay with a family outside the city. The plan was that each day, a local SCLC worker would pick up the SCOPE volunteers by car and drive the group to the site of voter registration activity for that day. Voter registration work would take place both in downtown Savannah and in Black neighborhoods outside the city. At the end of each workday, all of the student volunteers would be driven back to their host homes. Because the workers would be staying in different areas, they would not have many opportunities to socialize with other SCOPE workers on weeknights. On weekends, however, everyone was free to get together.

As mentioned, each volunteer was required to pay their host family $10 per week for room and board. If possible, a higher amount would be appreciated, they were told. SCOPE would pay an additional $5 per week to each host family. The host families had been screened by SCLC and instructed to treat the volunteers "like family." For most host families, this would be the first time that a White person had been inside their homes. At first the hosts would probably be just as uncomfortable with the living situation as their SCOPE guests, but ideally this would change for both the host families and the students as the summer progressed.

Swan explained that although Savannah was probably safer than most of the other locations where SCOPE would be operating that summer, volunteers still needed to take certain precautions. Swan frankly told them that it would not take long for the White SCOPE students to be identified by local Whites as civil rights workers from the North. They therefore should expect to be subjected to verbal abuse. They might be called "northern agitators," "Yankee agitators," "carpetbaggers" and "N— lovers."[1] Swan told Iris that as a young white woman, she would likely hear even more offensive language involving sexual conduct with Black men. The workers would also be accused of being Communists, a charge commonly leveled against civil rights activists. King himself was often called a Communist. It also was not unknown for deprogramming groups, like the ones that gained attention a decade later involving the "Moonies," to be hired by parents who sought to "save" their children from participating in the civil rights movement. Swan warned Iris and Boyd not to go with anyone who claimed to have been hired by their parents to bring them home. The KKK sometimes used this ruse to kidnap and terrorize civil rights workers. Additionally, in some circumstances, a volunteer would be told that their parent had suffered a heart attack (possibly induced by the child's civil rights activity), and that they had been sent to take the child back home. Most of these people had no relationship with any family members of the worker; they were kidnappers looking to be paid a ransom. Swan also warned about gasoline stations, which were often hangouts for KKK members. A gasoline station where a group of White men were standing around was not a safe place to use the bathroom or buy cigarettes (neither Iris nor Boyd smoked, but they got the point).

Swan first dropped Boyd off at his host family's home, a modest house in a Black section near downtown. He then drove with Iris to where she would be staying, in a Black section outside the city. Initially, Swan drove through parts of Savannah that looked much the same as some of the poorer Black sections that Iris had seen in Philadelphia, especially the neighborhood around Temple University. At a certain point, however, they crossed into an area that looked different. The streets were unpaved, just dirt, with dust flying up behind the car as they drove. Many of the houses rested on cinder blocks, with no cement foundations, something Iris had never seen in Philadelphia. The homes were sided with wood planks, not brick, stone, or aluminum siding. Many had broken windows. She saw outhouses in the back and chickens and pigs in the yards.

As they drove through this area that looked so unfamiliar to Iris, she saw a large building up ahead. When she asked about it, Swan told her that it was a paper bag factory. Many of the local residents worked there. After passing the factory, Swan parked the car on the side of a dirt road. "This is your new home," he told Iris. It was a wooden shack with a porch in the front. When Iris exited the car, she remembered being struck by two things. First, the weather. It was extremely hot and humid. She had experienced heat and humidity in Philadelphia during the summers, but this was a whole other matter. Second, a thick stench hung in the air, a horrible odor that made Iris shake her head and scrunch up her nose. It reminded her of the oil refineries near the Philadelphia airport, but it was much worse. When Iris mentioned the odor, Swan told her, "You'll get used to it. It's from the paper bag factory."[2]

A mother and two teenage daughters lived in Iris's host home. She could not recall their names when I met with her years later. No father, husband, or any males lived there. Unlike some other houses in the area, this one had an indoor bathroom with a toilet and bathtub, electricity, and a wringer washer. Clothes were dried on a line in the backyard. The mother worked as a domestic helper at several homes in a White section of Savannah. She took a bus to work. Her daughters were in high school and currently on summer break. They mostly stayed around the house during the day. The house had two bedrooms, one for the mother and one for the daughters. There were three twin-size mattresses on the floor in the daughters' bedroom. Iris slept on one of those mattresses. There was a radio in the living room, but no television in the house.

Iris's payment of $10 per week covered not only her room but also her meals. During the week she ate breakfast at the house before being picked up by a local SCOPE driver to do voter registration work.

At first she ate only scrambled eggs for breakfast, but eventually she added cornbread and grits to her morning fare. Although it was offered, Iris never ate bacon. Dinner typically included fried chicken, rice, collard greens, and corn bread. After dinner she would go with her two "host sisters" to hang out at a jukebox joint where she was the only White person. Everyone was extremely friendly, and after some initial shyness, she felt comfortable with the locals, who teased her about her lack of interest in drinking alcohol. The group had a special affection for a locally made moonshine, served in mason jars. After numerous polite refusals, Iris finally agreed to have a taste. Not surprisingly, she could barely get it down, and she ended up spitting most of it out. Everyone had a good-natured laugh over this. Near the jukebox hangout, another family lived with five children. Their house had a large porch on which people congregated. Iris would sometimes go there and socialize. She felt very comfortable with the locals, probably more so than with her neighbors in Northeast Philadelphia, with whom she rarely spoke. What amazed her the most was the generosity of the people of all ages in her host neighborhood. The people were very poor, yet they were willing to share whatever they had. Years later, when we spoke, Iris remembered being "moved by their poverty." She felt bad that they had so little. It was rumored that if a White employer learned that a Black employee was hosting a civil rights worker, that employee would be fired, but nevertheless her hosts were "fearless" in their hospitality. She told me that she wished she could remember their names to thank them.

Going to church was an important way to gain acceptance within the community, and Iris attended church with her host family every Sunday. She also enjoyed the meet-and-greet time after services. She made sure to wear her Sunday finest to church.[3] She was fascinated by the singing at church services as well as the powerful sermons the ministers delivered. She remarked on these sermons' length, much longer than those given by rabbis at Jewish services.

As per the rules discussed at the SCOPE orientation, Iris always wore modest outfits, usually a long dress. Around the neighborhood, she sometimes wore denim overalls over a long-sleeved cotton shirt. Overalls were popular in the neighborhood, and she bought hers at a local store. She wore her medium-length hair pulled back, often covered with a bandanna or wide-brimmed hat. She usually wore black sneakers or black flat shoes, which needed regular cleaning because the dirt streets turned to mud whenever it rained, which was often; strong rainstorms were common.

During their first week in Savannah, Iris and Boyd worked together setting up the SCOPE downtown office. A SCLC driver picked Iris up around 10:00 a.m., and Boyd thirty minutes or so later. They were driven to the SCOPE office, where they did some administrative work. Iris learned how to work the mimeograph machine to print voter registration brochures and other materials, while Boyd assembled a few desks, chairs, and bookshelves. They did not work very hard or long, and they took long lunch breaks. No later than 3:00 p.m., they would be driven back to their host homes. No voter registration activity took place that first week.

Once again, Iris and Boyd felt frustrated with how little they were accomplishing. They shared their feelings with J. T. Johnson, head of the Savannah office, who explained that SCOPE activity in Savannah would be slow going. First, no other SCOPE workers had arrived. He expected them to do so the following week. Moreover, he told them frankly, some in the civil rights community in Savannah were not all that supportive of SCOPE. They had worked hard alongside Hosea Williams in a successful voter registration drive the previous year, and they feared that SCOPE's presence might antagonize the White leadership, which had taken a mostly hands-off approach the year before. There also was concern that SCOPE workers would stir up emotions that might lead to trouble. The workers the summer before had all been from the Savannah area. The sight of White students from northern states soliciting Black people to register on the city's streets might ignite tensions not displayed for some time. Some local Black leaders worried that a misstep by some inexperienced White northern college student who did not understand either the Black or White communities in Savannah could erase the gains they had achieved the summer before. Johnson said he understood that Iris and Boyd were "fired up" and "ready to make a difference," but that they needed to be patient.

After this discussion, Johnson disclosed that he was leaving Savannah: SCLC had reassigned him to Crawfordsville, Georgia, to organize demonstrations to protest segregated public facilities there.

He would take some of the SCLC workers from Savannah with him. This news further disappointed Iris and Boyd, making them feel that the SCOPE project in Savannah was a low priority for SCLC. Their initial reaction to being assigned to the city now seemed justified. They felt a little better, however, when Johnson let them know that Swan had been named acting director. They liked Swan, but still, the "acting" part of his title indicated that he too might be transferred at any time.

On Saturday, Iris and Boyd took a bus to the beach on Hilton Head Island. They enjoyed the day, but both openly questioned why they had volunteered for SCOPE. Both had alienated their families, and for what? So far, they had done nothing to help wage the fight for racial injustice. They hoped in earnest that things would change when the other SCOPE volunteers arrived. Iris spent the next day, Sunday, attending church and socializing on a neighbor's porch. Later that day, Swan called her to tell her that she should be ready to "get to work." The other SCOPE volunteers had arrived, and the voter registration activities would begin.

On Monday, when Iris arrived at the SCOPE office, which she and Boyd had organized the week before, she met several new people. First, there was "Big Lester" Hankerson. Big Lester was a SCLC worker, well known in the movement, assigned to work in Savannah with SCOPE that summer.[4] Iris remembered him as "always on the scene" helping the volunteers identify potential registrants to convince them to go to the courthouse to register. As his nickname implied, Big Lester was a physically large man, one easily recognizable in the community when he walked down the street. He was also well liked and enjoyed talking with everyone he met. "He had a special charisma," Iris told me.

That summer in Savannah, one of Big Lester's roles was driver of the "Ballot Bus," a 1949 Packard limousine SCLC had acquired in 1963 as part of an earlier registration drive. Many people mistook the big car as a funeral hearse. The limousine's original shiny black paint was now faded, and several slogans painted in white adorned it. On the hood was painted "Free Rides, No Excuses." Above the front windshield were the words "Ballot Bus." Both sides were emblazoned "Register to Vote." The Ballot Bus had seating for eight, with space for three in the front row, two in rear-facing seats in a middle row, and three more in the rear row. It made quite an impression as it drove around Savannah, in stark contrast to most of the vehicles that SCLC's civil rights workers used for its voter registration activities, which were purposely kept inconspicuous to avoid vandalism.

During the voter registration drives in Savannah in 1963 and 1964, the Ballot Bus had been used to drive people to the Chatham County courthouse to register. But when the SCOPE program gained possession of the Ballot Bus in the summer of 1965, though it was still used occasionally to drive potential voters to the courthouse, by far its greatest use was as transportation for SCOPE workers. Every morning Big Lester would make the rounds, picking up each SCOPE worker at their host families' homes. He would then drive the group either to the SCOPE downtown office or to numerous canvass locations throughout Chatham County. During the day, Big Lester would drive around, checking on the SCOPE workers he'd dropped off to see if they had anyone who needed a ride to the courthouse. At the end of the day, by 4:00 p.m., he would get everyone back in the Ballot Bus and return them to their host homes. Riding around Savannah in the big, rather crazy car was fun for the group, although at times they felt a little nervous about how conspicuous they were in it. Iris spent a lot of time riding in the Ballot Bus because her host family lived farther from downtown than did the others. She was usually the first to be picked up and the last to be dropped off. The SCOPE volunteers felt that a lot of time was wasted driving around from host house to host house, time that could have been better spent working on voter registration. Still, it was fun riding in that vehicle!

Iris and Boyd were happy that ten other students had joined them in Savannah. None of the newcomers had attended orientation because of scheduling issues with their final exams. Though Iris was friendly with the others, she remained closest to Boyd. This was mostly because the others had arrived with friends from their hometowns or colleges. Among the group, only Iris and Boyd had joined SCOPE knowing no one else. With twelve volunteers in place, Swan held a group meeting in which all the volunteers introduced themselves, and he explained the plans for the voter registration work. Each volunteer would distribute informational flyers and sample registration forms to potential voters. At the end of each day, every worker had to complete a daily activity report that listed the name, address, and telephone number of each person they had spoken to about registering. The report should indicate whether the person agreed to register. If so, were there any special situations that needed attention? Here workers might note that a potential voter "needs transportation," "needs babysitter," "can't read or write," or "will help get others to register." Most days, the group would be working in Black neighborhoods outside of the downtown business district, but this would not always be the case. Because many Black people worked in unskilled positions in downtown businesses or as domestics in the homes of White families located downtown, on some days the group would canvas Black voters in the downtown section.

Swan further explained that all voter registration work would be done while standing on the street. They would not be knocking on doors. If someone said that they were not interested in registering, the volunteers were instructed not to push but just respond, "I'll be here again if you change your mind." If someone replied that they were interested in registering, the SCOPE volunteer should give them a flyer and a sample registration form, then ask whether they wanted any help completing the form. An offer of a ride to the courthouse should come next. Swan explained that some people might want to register but be hesitant to try to do so because they had not succeeded in a previous attempt, most because they had flunked the literacy or civics test. Others might be so concerned about flunking the tests that they had never even tried to register. Swan explained that to register to vote in most southern states, the voter registrar in each county would ask questions that one needed to answer to the registrar's satisfaction. There were no set rules for what knowledge was required. There was no official list of questions, nor any official answers. The registrars also had total discretion to waive this requirement and not ask any questions of the applicant. The typical situation in southern states was that registrars only asked Black applicants these questions. Moreover, the questions they asked were usually ones that very few people, if any, could answer correctly. For example, a biography of Jimmy Carter by Jonathan Alter includes a list of thirty questions used to disenfranchise Black voters. In the 1960s Carter lived in the rural community of Plains, Georgia, not far from Savannah. Among the questions asked of Black—but not White—people were:

- What is the name of the clerk of the superior court?
- Describe how the habeas corpus clause of the US Constitution is applied in criminal cases heard in Georgia courts.
- Who was vice president during the administration of President [X]? (Usually a president from over fifty years before); and
- Explain the *N*th Amendment to the United States Constitution. (Usually one of the obscure amendments such as the Sixteenth, authorizing a federal income tax, or the Seventh, guaranteeing the right to a jury trial in civil cases where the value in controversy exceeded $20.)[5]

Swan also shared with the group a memorandum that Hosea Williams had sent to every location leader. Addressed to "All SCOPE Workers," the memorandum said that each volunteer should provide SCOPE with the telephone numbers of their host family so that "we can contact you both day or night . . . immediately upon request of our office." The memorandum also imposed the requirement that every week, every SCOPE chapter would send a summary of that week's activities to the Atlanta office.[6]

For the next few weeks, the Savannah group followed a regular schedule. Because of the number of stops the Ballot Bus had to make to transport everyone, voter registration work usually did not start until about 11:00 a.m. The SCOPE workers would stand on the street within sight of each other. The weather was very hot and very humid; the word *steamy* best describes a Savannah summer. The SCOPE workers took frequent breaks for water and to cool off under trees. Many were drenched in sweat. To add to the discomfort, thunderstorms frequently occurred in the afternoons, which served to limit the length of the working day. The typical amount of time spent on the street trying to get people to register averaged between two and four hours per day. Before taking the volunteers back to their host homes, the Ballot Bus took them to the SCOPE office to complete the daily activity reports required by SCLC headquarters.

Each day followed a similar pattern for Iris. Wearing a long skirt and a wide-brimmed white straw hat, she stood on the street carrying a clipboard with information sheets on voter registration and sample registration forms. When she saw a potential Black voter, she would walk up to them and say, "Good morning [or afternoon]. My name is Iris Geller. I'm working with the Southern Christian Leadership Conference trying to get people to register to vote. Are you registered?" If the answer was yes, Iris would say "Thank you. Do you know anyone who is not registered to vote?" If they did, Iris would give the person an information sheet and a sample registration application to relay. She would say that she and others from SCLC would be on the street for the next month if the person's friend had any questions. Some people that Iris approached told her that everyone they knew had registered the past summer when Hosea Williams led a voter registration drive. In this case, Iris would reply with something like, "That's great. I know Mr. Williams."

If the person that Iris approached told her that they were not registered to vote, Iris would ask if they were interested in doing so. If they indicated any measure of interest, Iris would give them the information sheet, offer to assist them in completing the application, and ask if they would like a ride to the courthouse in the Ballot Bus. If someone expressed any concern over their ability to pass the civics test, Iris would discuss some sample questions with which she had been provided by SCLC, which did its best to maintain a bank of questions that had been asked to others.

Unfortunately, very few of the unregistered people with whom Iris interacted expressed any desire to register. Although some did speak briefly with Iris about registering, most of them just walked away without saying anything when they heard Iris's purpose in asking. The next largest group were people who took an information flyer without saying anything to her, but then deposited the flyer in the nearest trash can. In these cases, Iris would retrieve the flyer from the trash to reuse. Then there were those who stopped and told Iris that although they "might" be interested in registering to vote, they were concerned about doing so. These concerns stemmed from various reasons, including: (1) Their employer had threatened to fire them if they tried to register; (2) Everyone they knew who had tried to register had flunked the voting registration tests, so it would be useless to apply; (3) They could not read; (4) They had been threatened with violence by White people if they registered; and (5) They had received threatening calls warning them not to register to vote. Iris had been instructed, as had all SCOPE workers, not to push back on these reasons. The proper response was, "If you change your mind, I'll be around to help."

Some people told Iris that they had no interest whatsoever in voting. They said they considered voting a waste of time because it would not make any difference in their lives or the lives of anyone in their community. Others said that even if they did register and vote, White election officials would not count their ballot. They had never known of any Black political officeholders. They were not going to register to vote just to help elect some White candidate who had no interest in helping the Black community. Iris also heard stories that if a Black person did register to vote, their White employer would vote himself, using the employee's name at the polls. When Iris asked how the employer got away with doing this, she was told that nothing ever happened to the employer because the employee was afraid to complain. Moreover, any such complaint would not be taken seriously by White voting officials.

Iris heard some say they were not interested in registering because they could not afford to pay the poll taxes used in southern states to keep Black people from voting. Although the Twenty-Fourth Amendment to the US Constitution, which was ratified on January 23, 1964, provided that voting rights could not be denied by reason of failure to pay any poll tax or other tax, this amendment at first was applied only to federal elections for the president, US senators, and members of the House of Representatives. This would remain the case until 1966, when the US Supreme Court held in *Harper v. Virginia Board of Elections* that all poll taxes, including ones for local elections, were outlawed.[7] Again, the SCOPE workers were told not to argue the validity of the reasons people had for not wanting to register.

Standing on the hot and humid streets of Savannah trying to get people to register to vote proved tiring and frustrating. Most days, nothing was accomplished. The highlight of the day might be someone merely stopping and talking for a couple minutes. Among the group of twelve SCOPE workers in Savannah, the general feeling was that the project was not well organized or planned. All agreed that it was less rewarding than expected. A few of the volunteers decided to leave after a couple weeks. Not much was getting done, and the weather was unbearable. Iris and Boyd discussed leaving, but again decided to stay. They had both alienated their parents by joining SCOPE,[8] and they did not want to admit that their decision might not have been worth the battle. Neither had yet to register a single person, but maybe things would change.

The owners of businesses on the streets on which the SCOPE workers stood were not pleased by the voter registration activity. They were concerned that others might interpret the SCOPE workers' presence in front of their business as the owner's support of SCOPE's goals. They worried about the possibility of confrontations between local Whites and civil rights workers. Owners also feared that SCOPE's presence would discourage customers from entering their stores. SCOPE workers routinely just moved down the street whenever they got a complaint from a business. Fortunately, in Savannah that summer, no violence or arrests involving SCOPE workers occurred.

Serious tensions, including violence, did however arise in other SCOPE locations. On July 1, Rev. Ralph Abernathy, SCLC's vice president at large, issued a press release for general publication by the national media. It stated that some student volunteers and local Black people engaged in voter registration projects throughout the South were being subjected to "sinister harassments and brutal intimidations." It was "significant that this brutality campaign began at the same time that SCLC launched its SCOPE project." The press release continued: "College students working in the SCOPE project are withstanding the brunt of the most vicious attacks imaginable." Examples of violence against SCOPE workers were then listed: An eighteen-year-old SCOPE worker from San Francisco was arrested and badly beaten in Camden, Alabama. He required hospitalization. In Monroe County, Alabama, several SCOPE workers were "forced to flee the county and abandon their voter registration work by county and local police officials." In Americus, Georgia, two SCOPE workers were cut by glass when local White youths "resented their presence at a segregated state park and hurled bricks and bottles against their car window." Abernathy's press release added, "We firmly believe that the vicious treatment of the local Negroes and our voter registration workers is symptomatic of a sick society in which Negro citizens are denied the right to vote for elected officials. . . . We in SCLC would like to tell the parents and friends of our SCOPE volunteers that they too are remembered in our prayers. We want you to know that your concern for their welfare and safety away from home also is our concern. These dedicated volunteers have proven their commitment to the cause of human dignity by laboring under a sweltering sun and often in the shadow of personal danger for the advancement of an oppressed people."[9]

When this press release was read to the SCOPE workers at the Savannah office, Iris wondered if her parents would see it in the newspapers. If they did read it, they would have a wrong impression of her experience in Savannah. She decided, however, not to contact them to tell them not to worry about her. She was unsure whether they even cared. They had most likely stopped worrying about her after she left for Atlanta without having been honest with them. Other SCOPE workers did decide to contact their parents to tell them that they were safe, and that no SCOPE workers had been attacked in Savannah. Their main complaint was boredom, not violence.

The Abernathy press release started a conversation among the group about being assigned to Savannah. Iris was among those who envied those workers in locations that had "more action." Others said they had no problem being in a safe place. Some questioned whether this press release accurately described the dangers faced by SCOPE workers or whether it had picked a few isolated examples in an effort to gain support, especially financial support, for SCOPE. Swan then told the group about what SCLC called "incident reports" that each location was required to file with the main Atlanta office whenever anything threatening or violent occurred.[10] He had not discussed these reports with the group before now because there had been no such problems in Savannah. He did, however, tell them that he had received copies of such reports from other locations covering incidents up to July 1. He read some of them to the group. For example, in Sumter County, Georgia, an integrated group including SCOPE workers had been harassed, threatened, and their car damaged. In Wilcox County, Alabama, a county sheriff told a White owner of a café in a Black section not to serve White SCOPE workers. In White Hill County, Georgia, a SCOPE worker was threatened by a White man with a gun. In Camden, Alabama, eighteen people were arrested in the SCOPE office for possession of materials urging a boycott of several White-owned businesses. In Wilcox County, Alabama, SCOPE workers were warned that if they were found in the church where their office was located after dark, they would be arrested for public nuisance or burglary. There was even an incident report involving harassment by a local Black resident in Richmond County, Georgia. A Black neighbor of a Black family hosting a White SCOPE worker called the police to have the SCOPE worker evicted from the neighborhood. The host family withdrew from the program, and the worker was moved to a different section of town.

As the summer progressed, the reported incidents grew more serious.[11] For example, during the month of July, the following incidents were reported to the Atlanta office: In Barbour County, Alabama, a White driver of a pickup truck tried to run down a SCOPE worker but did not succeed in causing any injury. In Marengo County, Alabama, a deputy sheriff choked a SCOPE worker. In Wilcox County, Alabama, three cars driven by SCOPE workers were shot at by White men. The SCOPE workers were then forced off the highway by a White man in a pickup truck who brandished a rifle. In Taliaferro County, Georgia, SCOPE workers were threatened with injury if they did not leave town by the next day. In Geneva County, Georgia, a SCOPE worker was threatened with arrest for questioning why a Black college student had flunked the voter registration test. In Laurens County, Georgia, SCOPE workers attempted to integrate a White Baptist church by bringing along several Black youths. The entire group was teargassed. One youth was beaten. In Newberry County, South Carolina, a SCOPE worker was beaten by three White youths. In Clayton, Alabama, a SCOPE worker was attacked by three White men. His car windows were broken, and the worker was dragged out of his car. The worker was able to run away. Local police watched this happen but did nothing. In Sussex County, Virginia, two SCOPE workers were threatened by a White man with a shotgun. In Houston County, Georgia, a SCOPE volunteer was attacked by a White man while canvassing.

The incident reports filed in August included the following: In Allendale County, South Carolina, SCOPE workers and local Black people were arrested for refusing to leave the courthouse after the registrar's office closed with two hundred people waiting to register. Only fifty-five applications were processed all day. In Crenshaw County,

Alabama, two SCOPE workers were beaten on the street by a group of White men. In Bibb County, Georgia, a SCOPE worker was beaten by two White men when he tried to take a Black person into a restaurant that did not serve Black people. In Hale County, Alabama, two SCOPE workers were attacked while protesting the refusal of a bloodmobile to serve a community blood drive in a Black area. In Butler County, Alabama, SCOPE workers were teargassed during a sit-in to protest voter registration practices. In Barbour County, Alabama, shots were fired into a local SCOPE worker's house. In Gadsden County, Florida, a SCOPE worker was beaten while walking with others to the voter registration office. In Berkeley County, South Carolina, two SCOPE workers were beaten while trying to integrate a restaurant along with local Black people. In the same county, a host home for a SCOPE worker was shot up. The same thing happened at a store where the SCOPE office was located. In Taylor County, Georgia, a SCOPE worker was beaten. In Barbour County, Alabama, SCOPE workers were arrested for protesting the limited hours the voter registration office was open. In Orangeburg, South Carolina, a SCOPE worker was arrested for helping people register to vote. No charges were filed, but she was kept in one jail cell with fifteen other women for several hours.

These incident reports filed with SCLC's Atlanta office most likely describe only a small number of the "incidents" that SCOPE workers faced. The warnings that SCLC gave to prospective volunteers during on-campus recruitment interviews and at the Atlanta orientation had not been false alarms. These warnings were the product of years of experience of SCLC and other civil rights organizations working in the South. Fortunately, unlike during Freedom Summer in 1964, no one from SCOPE was killed. The courage of the SCOPE workers in the midst of such hatred was remarkable. Although Iris had demonstrated courage in joining SCOPE, her experience in Savannah did not involve the dangers faced by SCOPE workers in other locations.

CHAPTER 5

Americus, Georgia

BOTH IRIS AND BOYD WERE frustrated with their posting in Savannah. Despite their best efforts, they were unsuccessful in registering any new voters. Iris felt that the lack of organization in Savannah hurt their efforts. And in truth, Iris, Boyd, and the other SCOPE volunteers in Savannah did not receive much community support. At other SCOPE locations, church groups and local activists welcomed the students and had plans in place for their involvement in voter registration drives. When Iris and Boyd showed up in Savannah, the general reaction from the local leaders was "What are you doing here?" Also, J. T. Johnson's transfer away from Savannah hampered the effort there. During the second week of July, however, Iris and Boyd received welcome news. Hosea Williams told them that he wanted them to leave Savannah and go to Americus, Georgia. Hosea said that Americus had the potential to become the "next Selma," and that they needed "reinforcements" there. Iris and Boyd jumped at the chance to leave Savannah. Iris was especially excited about the opportunity to see "real action" in a rural Georgia town. She remembered that trouble in Americus had been mentioned in several incident reports.

Americus, in southwest Georgia, lies about two hundred miles west from Savannah's Atlantic coast location. Americus is only ten miles east of Plains, Georgia, hometown of President Jimmy Carter. Americus had a history of racial strife. In 1961, Martin Luther King was jailed there.[1] Like most rural southern towns in the early 1960s, Americus was racially divided. Black people attended segregated and inferiorly funded schools. Public bathrooms were segregated by race, and there were separate "Colored" and "White" water fountains. Black people could not eat or drink at any public lunch counter. They were allowed to purchase items from local stores (all White-owned), but they were forbidden from trying on clothing or returning purchases. There were no Black employees at the grocery stores despite serving a large Black clientele. At the time, Sumter County had a population of about twenty-five thousand people, thirteen thousand of whom lived in Americus. Slightly more than 50 percent of the town's population was Black. Median annual income was about $1,200 for Black people compared to $5,100 for Whites.[2] Only about three hundred Black people in Americus were registered to vote in 1962.[3]

The sheriff in Americus was Fred Chappell, who had a deserved reputation as a racist. Martin Luther King once described him as the "meanest man in the world."[4] His power in Americus went virtually unchecked. Moreover, his family members controlled many of the other official positions in town, including the county clerk's office which oversaw voter registration. Other relatives served as postmaster, county commissioner, state public service commissioner, and state police officer. The mayor of Americus, T. Griffin Walker, consistently refused to appoint any biracial committee to consider race relations in the city. Chief of Police Ross M. Chambliss also held the same racist views as Sheriff Chappell and Mayor Walker.

Americus, as mentioned, was one of the locations to which SCLC had sent SCOPE workers after the orientation in Atlanta. The Student Nonviolent Coordinating Committee (SNCC) had been working in Americus for several years before SCOPE workers arrived. In 1961 SNCC had created the Southwest Georgia Project in nearby Albany, Georgia, under the direction of Charles Sherrod, who many consider one of the founding fathers of SNCC. In 1962 in his capacity as a field secretary for SNCC, Sherrod sent several SNCC workers to Americus to work with local Black leaders. Americus already had an active community of local activists, including church officials and students. At first SNCC focused its efforts on voter registration. They held mass meetings at several churches, and students canvassed neighborhoods. This voter registration drive proved a success, as the Black voter roll increased after 1962.

Come 1963, however, racial tensions increased. In July, eleven young Black people went to a local movie cinema, the Martin Theater on

Forsyth Street, and tried to buy admission tickets at a ticket window marked "Whites Only." The ticket agent called police, who ordered the youths to leave the area. When they refused to disperse, the police arrested them, charging them with disorderly conduct. These arrests led to regularly held demonstrations protesting police brutality and segregation of public facilities.[5] Among those participating in the marches was John Lewis, now chair of SNCC. The marches attracted large numbers of young Black students.

In August 1963 three SNCC workers, Don Harris, Ralph Allen, and John Perdew, along with Congress of Racial Equality (CORE) worker Zev Aelony, were beaten and burned with cattle prods while participating in a demonstration on Cotton Avenue. All four men were arrested and charged with multiple crimes, including inciting riot, battery on a police officer, and, most seriously, sedition in violation of an 1871 Georgia anti-treason statute. The significance of the sedition charge was that it was punishable by death, and Georgia law prohibited bail for any capital offense. These activists became known as the Americus Four. They remained in jail for eighty-five days until a three-judge federal court ruled the Georgia anti-treason statute to be unconstitutional and ordered their release.[6]

SCOPE volunteers arrived in Americus on June 19 to live with their host families in the Black neighborhood on the north end of town. From the beginning, they faced harassment. White night riders drove through the Black neighborhood, throwing bricks, setting off firecrackers, and shooting bullets in the air. Although no SCOPE workers were injured, the host families expressed concern about the safety of the students they housed—as well as their own safety. Some SCOPE workers were moved to host family homes in areas considered safer.

At first the SCOPE workers in Americus focused their voter registration efforts on canvassing Black neighborhoods in and around town. In the evenings they attended mass meetings at churches, organized mostly by SNCC workers, often in conjunction with church leaders such as the Reverend Joseph Campbell, the pastor at Allen's Church. They also drove to rural areas outside of town to talk with sharecroppers who lived in "shotgun shacks." In general, they failed to help many people register to vote in Americus or the surrounding area. As in other places, some Black residents of Americus told the

SCOPE workers that they had tried to register before but had failed the literacy or citizenship tests and did not wish to face further humiliation. Others said they would not register because they were afraid of violence from KKK night riders. Still others worried about losing their job or being thrown off the land they farmed if they even attempted to register to vote.

For the most part, SCOPE workers in Americus tried to avoid trouble. When they were not talking with potential voters, they hung out at the Barnum Funeral Home, owned by local activist Mabel Barnum, who the SCOPE workers called Grandma. The student volunteers regularly attended church services and political meetings held at several churches. They were also welcome at the town's SNCC Freedom Center, established a couple years earlier. This center served as the headquarters for SNCC as well as a social hall for residents.

SCOPE workers did not, however, always manage to avoid trouble. For example, one day at the end of June, a group of student volunteers joined local Black teenagers in attempting to swim at a pool restricted to Whites. The entire group was denied entry. The matter ended when the young people left the pool area after being told that they would not be admitted. A more serious situation involved a car that had been loaned to the SCOPE workers. One day when a few of them were driving to a rural area outside Americus, White youths drove up alongside the SCOPE car and shot out the headlights and some of the windows. Luckily, no one was injured. The SCOPE workers reported the incident to the police, who did nothing about it.

The event that triggered Williams's call for SCOPE "reinforcements," and which had led Iris and Boyd to come to Americus, began with the death (from natural causes) of Justice of the Peace Cooper Bradley, a White man, on June 23. In a special election set to replace Bradley, two candidates filed for election: John Southwell, a White man, and Mary Kate Fishe Bell, a Black woman. Bell was the first Black person, man or woman, to run for public office in Sumter County since Reconstruction. SCOPE and SNCC began working around the clock for Bell's election, not only continuing to try to register new voters, but also telling those already registered to vote for Bell in the upcoming special election. Williams deemed the number of SCOPE workers already in Americus inadequate to put forth the campaign that seemed necessary to get Bell elected, so he ordered SCOPE workers from other areas, including Iris and Boyd, to report to Americus.

When they arrived from Savannah, Boyd and Iris were assigned housing. Boyd was told to stay at the Barnum Funeral Home, where he joined about a dozen other SCOPE men. All of them slept in sleeping bags on the floor of the parlor. Iris, like other female SCOPE workers, was placed with a host family in a Black neighborhood. The family with whom Iris lived had a two-story wooden house. SCOPE paid the host family $5 per week for Iris's room and board. By this time, Iris had become more accustomed to southern cooking. She enjoyed the rice, biscuits, chicken, and sweet potato pie her host family served her. Also living at Iris's host family house was a pet hog. The hog, whose name was Donny,[7] slept inside the house, and Iris, along with the family members, enjoyed petting and playing with Donny. One day, Iris realized that Donny was not around. The next day, when pork was served for dinner, Iris realized where Donny was.

Iris spent the next few weeks campaigning for Mary Kate Fishe Bell for justice of the peace, and found this type of work more satisfying than trying to get people to register to vote. She was now speaking with people who were already registered, committed to exercising their right to vote, and knew Bell personally—or at least knew someone who knew her personally. All Iris had to do was to urge them to vote on election day. Bell's candidacy created excitement among the Black voters that none had experienced in prior elections. Events surrounding the election, however, would lead to more racial strife.

On election day, candidate Bell, along with three other Black women, Lena Turner, Gloria Wise, and Mamie Campbell, went to the polls to vote. Even though the federal Civil Rights Act of 1964 prohibited racial discrimination in voting, Sumter County election laws required three lines for those waiting to vote—one line for White men, one line for White women, and one line for all Black voters. Bell and the other three Black women waited in the line marked "White Females." When they got to the front of the line and tried to enter the polling location, Sheriff Fred Chappell arrested all four and confined them in a jail cell in the Sumter County Courthouse. At a court hearing, bail was set at $1,000. Following the "Jail, No Bail" policy adopted by most in the civil rights movement, the four prisoners refused to post bond. By staying in jail, they hoped to draw attention to the unjustness of their arrests. In this they succeeded. Word spread of the women's arrests, and street demonstrations followed.[8] Marches were held every day for several weeks. On some days there were three marches, held at 12:00 noon, 6:00 p.m., and 10:00 p.m.. The marches usually started at the Friendship Baptist Church, moved to the Sumter County Courthouse, and then returned to the church. Initially, the sole demand of the protesters was the release of the four jailed women. Later, their goals expanded to address a broader range of racial discrimination in and around Americus. Participants in these marches were workers from SCOPE and SNCC, including their leaders Hosea Williams and John Lewis. The popular comedian and civil rights activist Dick Gregory also joined the cause in Americus. Iris participated regularly in these marches.

Besides marching, the protesters put out a call to boycott White-owned businesses in Americus that refused to hire Black employees even though their customers were primarily Black. This boycott threat made the local White business establishment very nervous, so much so that the Americus Merchants Association (AMA) offered to pay the $1,000 bail for each jailed woman.[9] The women refused the offer. The AMA urged the mayor to appoint a biracial community relations committee as a gesture of good faith to avoid economic boycotts. The mayor refused. Members of the AMA personally attended a meeting of civil rights activists at Friendship Baptist Church and pleaded with them to stop the marches and boycotts, explaining that they were trying their best to improve race relations in Americus. The AMA members received a kind reception at the meeting, but their request was unanimously rejected.

The racial atmosphere in Americus grew ever more threatening the longer the four women remained in jail. The marches grew in number and size. On July 23, eight local Black leaders met with city officials and businesspeople to discuss the concerns of the Black community relating to voting and employment. That night a crowd of about three hundred, including Iris, attended a mass rally at the church and then marched to the county courthouse, where the four women remained jailed. After the rally and march ended, a seventeen-year-old Black youth, E. G. Rogers, was shot while walking back to his home. Witnesses described the assailants as three White men in a green pickup truck. Fortunately, Rogers escaped serious injury. No arrests were made.

On July 24 candidate Bell and the other three jailed Black women issued a "Letter from the Sumter County Jail."[10] Their inspiration was Dr. King's famous 1963 letter from a Birmingham, Alabama, jail. In response to an open letter addressed to him from eight members of the clergy, urging him to abandon his direct action tactics as "unwise and untimely," King wrote that he was "gravely disappointed" with White moderates who seemed to place more emphasis on order than justice, adding that an "unjust law is no law at all."[11] In their own letter, the four jailed women explained that they were refusing to post bail to protest the unjustness of their arrest. They demanded that all charges against them be dropped, and that segregated voting lines be immediately abolished.

After the release of the letter from the Sumter County jail, Iris joined five hundred other marchers on the familiar route from the Friendship Baptist Church to the courthouse. The next day, more than eight hundred people marched along the same route. On July 26, marches commenced at noon and at 6:00 p.m. The number of marchers grew with each event. Williams continued to dispatch more SCOPE reinforcements to Americus from other locations. SNCC, too, sent more workers to Americus. Williams and Lewis announced that SCLC and SNCC would work together in Americus and coordinate their activities,[12] as they had done in Selma. As Williams had predicted, Americus was indeed developing into the "next Selma."

On the night of July 26, between five and eight hundred people marched from the Friendship Baptist Church to the courthouse, where they held a rally during which both Williams and Lewis spoke. Although Iris harbored some ill feelings toward Williams because of her bathroom-cleaning experience at the Freedom House, she could not squelch her pride that she knew him on a personal basis. How many other people at the rally could say that? On the other hand, Iris had never seen John Lewis, and she found herself mesmerized by his speech. What a wonderful speaker, she thought. In less than two months, Iris had seen and heard in person two of the greatest speakers of the civil rights movement—King at the SCOPE orientation in Atlanta, and Lewis in Americus.

After the rally at the courthouse, most of the crowd began to disperse and walk home. Suddenly, Iris heard gunshots and saw some people running. Fortunately, no one was injured. It may have just been someone shooting a gun into the air, not aimed at anyone, but it was still a sharp reminder of the risks involved in working as a civil rights activist in Americus. Rather than walking back to their host families' homes that night, Iris and most of the other SCOPE workers heeded the call from Williams to stay after the rally for an all-night vigil. Williams had told his SCOPE workers to bring sleeping bags and food and stay until the morning, and Lewis had told his SNCC workers the same. Most of those who intended to stay all night at the vigil were young workers from SCLC/SCOPE and SNCC. There were no speeches, just civil rights activists hanging out and enjoying themselves into the night.

About 2:00 a.m., Williams arrived and told everyone to go home. The White political and business leaders in Americus had grown especially nervous and had asked him to meet with them earlier that night. They told him they thought that the all-night vigil might well invite violence. Then they made him an offer: The mayor would form a biracial committee if Williams asked everyone to go home immediately. Williams had agreed, and was now telling those planning to stay all night to head home instead. Everyone, including Iris, followed his advice. The next day, however, the agreement to form a biracial committee collapsed; the city's White leaders had rejected Williams's two nominees for the committee, Sam Malone of SNCC and Lena Turner of SCOPE. The only thing the proposal accomplished was to end the previous night's vigil. No biracial committee was formed in Americus.[13]

After the agreement's collapse, Williams announced that there would be three marches that day, as well as another all-night vigil. Iris decided to skip the first two marches and attend only the third one, scheduled for 10:00 p.m. She also planned to stay afterward for the all-night vigil. At the 10:00 p.m. rally, most of the speeches concerned the demand for a biracial committee. Then trouble began. At about 11:30 p.m., a twenty-one-year-old White male resident of Americus, Andrew Whatley, was shot by two Black men near the courthouse where the rally was taking place.[14] Whatley was no stranger to racial hostilities in Americus. Two years earlier, while working as a projectionist at the Martin Theater, he had become involved in a confrontation with some Black youths who attempted to buy tickets at the "Whites Only" ticket window. Moreover, Whatley had been identified as a member of a White night riders' group that had terrorized Black neighborhoods in June, a few weeks earlier. Now, on this night, he was part of a group of about twelve White men throwing bricks, rocks, and bottles at cars driven by Blacks near the rally site, breaking car windows. Two Black men, Charles Lee Hopkins and Eddie Will Lamar, were in one of the cars hit by a brick. Hopkins responded by firing a gun at the car from which the brick had been thrown. Whatley, a passenger in the car, was hit by a bullet. He was taken by ambulance to a hospital in Albany, Georgia, where he died at about 3:00 a.m.[15]

When news of Whatley's death reached the organizers of the courthouse vigil, they announced that everyone should go home immediately. Iris and the other demonstrators carefully made their way back to their homes. All fully expected more violence to follow, so Williams and other leaders decided to cancel all marches and rallies the next day. Americus was eerily quiet and subdued that day as Iris and the other civil rights activists stayed near their home bases and tried to catch up on their sleep.

In the wake of Whatley's death, Hopkins and Lamar were both indicted for murder. Lamar agreed to plead guilty to voluntary manslaughter and received a sentence of five years in jail. Hopkins went to trial. He testified in his defense that he had been frightened when the car window by which he was seated was hit by a brick and shattered, and that he had responded by shooting "blindly" at the car in which Whatley was riding. After an all-White jury found Hopkins guilty of murder, the judge sentenced him to life in prison.

Amid these mass marches, all-night vigils, and incidents of racial violence, the US Department of Justice (DOJ) filed a lawsuit in federal district court for the Middle District of Georgia, *United States v. Chappell*, arguing that the segregated voting lines in Sumter County were illegal under the 1964 Civil Rights Act and in violation of the US Constitution. The fact that the DOJ was now involved was welcome news in Americus. It did not take the federal district court judge in Atlanta very long to issue his decision. A few days after the DOJ filed its lawsuit, the judge ruled that the segregated voting lines were illegal and issued an order enjoining their further use. He also ordered the immediate release from jail of Bell and the three other women.[16]

The release of the four women excited Iris and her fellow SCOPE and SNCC workers. They had won a tangible victory, but it did not resolve all the issues. One remaining matter was who should serve as justice of the peace. Even though the ballot count had revealed more votes cast for candidate Southwell, civil rights activists wanted Bell to be declared the winner due to the illegality of the election, and they filed a lawsuit to that effect. The federal district court judge, however, although reaffirming the illegality of the segregated voting lines, refused to set aside the election results. He based his ruling on the fact that there weren't enough registered Black voters eligible to vote in the special election to change the results, even if every one of them had voted for Bell. This decision was appealed to the US Court of Appeals for the Fifth Circuit, which reversed the lower court's decision and ordered the holding of a new election, but stopped short of naming Bell the justice of the peace. In the second contest, Southwell easily defeated Bell, and he was sworn in as the new justice of the peace.

Even after Bell's release from jail, issues such as better job opportunities for Black people, the hiring of Black workers in White-owned shops, the creation of a biracial committee to engage in meaningful dialogue on racial issues, and segregated churches remained pressing concerns in Americus. The activists decided that the mass meetings, marches, and other demonstrations should resume after the one-day pause following Whatley's death. As SCOPE activities slowed down in other towns, more SCOPE workers arrived in Americus to participate in the protests. Iris felt like a veteran since she had been in Americus for several weeks.

For the past several years, there had been protests in Americus over the lack of Black employees in White-owned businesses in Black neighborhoods. The city's grocery stores seemed like good targets for protests because none of them had any Black cashiers, shelf stackers, or employees in any capacity. Some suggested boycotting grocery stores, but the residents' need for food drowned out such calls. Boycotts against less essential businesses with no Black employees were suggested. For the most part, the protests and boycotts did not succeed. There were limited choices in Americus's Black neighborhoods, whose residents had little choice but to do business with White-owned stores, with or without Black workers. The activism surrounding the justice of the peace special election in the summer of 1965, along with the infusion of SCOPE and SNCC workers into Americus, however, created a new opportunity to deal with economic issues along with the political ones.

On July 31 nineteen civil rights workers, including SCOPE and SNCC members, picketed outside the Colonial Supermarket. Among the picketers from SCOPE was Boyd, but not Iris. After the protesters marched outside the store for only a short time, the manager of the store insisted they stop picketing. They agreed to stop picketing, but then they all walked into the store, took shopping carts, and walked up and down the aisles singing songs from the civil rights movement such as "We Shall Overcome." In so doing, they were holding what they called a "shop-in," as opposed to a "sit-in." They pretended to shop by taking items off the shelf, reading labels, and then either returning them to the shelf or placing them in their carts. After about thirty minutes, the manager of the store told them to check out and pay for the items in their carts or leave. The protesters refused to do so and simply continued their shop-in. At this point, the manager locked the doors of the store and put up a Closed sign. Although he continued to ask the demonstrators to leave, the protest went on for two hours, after which the demonstrators left and the store was reopened for business. All had occurred peacefully.

The shop-in demonstrators, including Boyd, then walked a short distance to another grocery store, the Kwik Chek, intending to stage another shop-in. The manager of the Kwik Chek, Carl Fox, having heard of what had just occurred at Colonial Supermarket, locked the doors when he saw the group walking toward his store. When the demonstrators arrived at the Kwik Chek and found the doors locked, they knocked and asked Fox, who they could see inside the store, to let them in. Fox refused to do so, telling the group that the store was closed. By this time, news of the shop-in had spread. As Boyd and his fellow demonstrators stood outside the Kwik Chek, a group of Whites, mostly males in their twenties, arrived and started yelling racial slurs. At this point, Americus police and Georgia State Police officers arrived. Both the local and state law enforcement officers, however, kept their distance from both groups and did not interfere with the name-calling. The hostile group members soon escalated things and began to attack the demonstrators, hitting them with fists, clubs, and pistols. For more than five minutes the police officers just watched as the angry White mob badly beat the outnumbered demonstrators. Horrified, Boyd, who had not been attacked, most likely because he was White, ran to the police and screamed at them to do something to stop the beatings. As Boyd beseeched one of the Georgia State Police officers, he felt a strong blow to the back of his head. Another officer had taken his billy club and smacked Boyd with it. Boyd fell to the ground, where he lay in tremendous pain in a semiconscious state, his blood pooling on the sidewalk. Local and state police officers now intervened and stopped the assault on the demonstrators, many of whom were bleeding. Boyd was the most seriously injured. Going in and out of consciousness, he was placed in a car and driven to the Barnum Funeral Home. His fellow activists soon decided, however, that they needed to take Boyd to the Sumter County Hospital emergency room. Upon examination at the hospital, the doctor said that Boyd would have to see a neurologist. Because there were no neurologists in Sumter County, Boyd had to be transferred to an Atlanta hospital for examination there. His coworkers drove him to Atlanta in a SCOPE car. He lay semiconscious during the three-hour drive to a hospital in Atlanta, where a neurologist treated him. News of what happened spread among the SCOPE workers throughout Americus and to the other locations. The extent of Boyd's injuries was yet unknown, but rumors began to spread that he had been seriously injured, perhaps paralyzed, and possibly soon to die. Iris was understandably shaken. Her best friend during the SCOPE summer had been brutally assaulted, taken to a hospital in Atlanta, and might not survive.

After the attack on Boyd, Iris considered leaving Americus, traveling to Savannah for her personal belongings, and then returning to Philadelphia, Pennsylvania. She was not truly interested in returning to her parents' house, where she was not sure she was welcome, but the violence in Americus seemed too much to bear without Boyd. After some thought, she decided to remain in Americus and await further news of her friend. The next day, an article appeared in *The New York Times* that greatly concerned Iris and her fellow SCOPE workers.[17] The article, which recounted the events at the Kwik Chek, stated that Boyd had suffered "brain damage." This vague diagnosis made everyone fear the worst for their coworker. Fortunately, Boyd had only suffered a concussion and made a full recovery within a couple weeks.[18]

After his discharge from the Atlanta hospital, Boyd did not return to Americus or Savannah. Rather, he stayed in Atlanta and moved into the SCLC Freedom House, where he and Iris had stayed after the SCOPE orientation. His belongings from Savannah were sent to Atlanta. Hosea Williams personally offered Boyd a job working for SCLC in Atlanta at a salary of $15 per week plus room and board. Boyd was happy to accept Williams's offer. He worked at the SCLC headquarters, preparing materials for SCLC chapters around the country. After about one month, Boyd was transferred to Emporia, Virginia. A Black candidate running for a local office in Emporia had asked SCLC for assistance in increasing the Black vote in his district. But when Boyd arrived in Emporia, the candidate told SCLC that he did not want a White civil rights worker to help his campaign. Now SCLC sent Boyd to work on voter registration in Hopewell, Virginia. He stayed with SCLC until November, when he left Hopewell and returned to South Bend, Indiana. Once there, however, Boyd did not re-enroll at the University of Notre Dame. Instead, he took a job as a salesman at a shoe store near campus. He stayed in this job for about a year and then moved back to his home state of Mississippi to attend Mississippi State University. After graduating college, he attended Lutheran Seminary, even though he had been raised Catholic. Ordained as a Lutheran minister, he served several churches until his retirement.

Iris remained in Americus after Boyd suffered the attack. The city now faced the aftermath of the violence at the Kwik Chek. No one was arrested for the attacks on the grocery store demonstrators. No state trooper was ever named as the one who attacked Boyd. In fact, the Georgia State Police denied that any of its officers had done anything improper, including denying that they had stood by and allowed the white mob to attack those outside the Kwik Chek.

The Sunday after the events at the Kwik Chek was a quiet day. Most of the civil rights activists, including Iris, attended church services. But on Monday, more demonstrations started. In fact, three of them were held that day. At 9:00 a.m., the first group of about twenty people marched together to the same Kwik Chek. When the store manager saw the marchers coming down the street, he locked the doors. The demonstrators stood outside the front door on the sidewalk, just as Boyd and his fellow demonstrators had done a couple days before. The store manager called the police to have the demonstrators arrested for trespassing on the sidewalk in front of his store—even though the sidewalk was public property. The police arrived and arrested nine demonstrators, seven Black and two White. At 10:00 a.m., a second group of demonstrators arrived at the food market, and the same set of events played out, with fourteen people arrested this time. Then, at 2:00 p.m., a third group marched to the Kwik Chek store. This group included Iris. In this third round, the police made no arrests, and the group dispersed after about thirty minutes. Later that day, all those arrested in the first two groups were released from jail with all charges dropped. That same day, small groups also picketed in front of the Colonial Supermarket and Piggly Wiggly grocery stores but did so without any incidents or arrests.

As the week progressed, more demonstrations were planned with Williams ordering more SCOPE workers to Americus. About thirty new SCOPE workers were brought from Macon, Crawfordville, and Albany. Marches were held every day. Although the protesters continued to picket grocery stores, they made no further attempts to hold any shop-ins. Protests did spread to White-owned stores other than grocery stores, but without incident.

The next places targeted for direct action protest in Americus were its segregated churches.[19] The Presbyterian, Episcopal, and Catholic churches in Americus were integrated, but the city's two largest congregations, the First Baptist Church and the First Methodist Church, barred Black people from worship. Over the years, local Black people had attempted to attend services at these churches but had always been refused entry. The energy brought to Americus by SCOPE and SNCC workers, however, created a new push for the integration of these two churches. On August 1, local Black residents, along with civil rights workers, attempted to integrate First Methodist. That same day, SNCC workers, led by John Lewis, went to First Baptist. At the respective churches, the groups were denied entry. In response, both groups knelt and prayed before departing. During the first week of August, SNCC and SCOPE brought more workers to Americus. On Sunday, August 8, two groups of integrated civil rights workers again sought entry to the two segregated churches. This time, leaders of both churches called the police, who made numerous arrests. At First Baptist, police arrested thirteen civil rights workers, seven Black and six White. Among those arrested was John Lewis. All thirteen of them were charged with the crime of "interfering with Divine worship." At First Methodist, eight protesters came under arrest, four Black and four White, and were charged with the same "interference with Divine worship" crime, as well as trespassing. All twenty-one people arrested on August 8 at the two churches spent the night in jail. The next day, those arrested at First Methodist were released when the church dropped the charges. Those arrested at First Baptist spent a second night in jail. On Tuesday, a hearing was held before Justice of the Peace Southwell (the White man who had won the special election). The defendants were all released on bond in amounts that varied between $300 and $600. Charges against everyone arrested were eventually dropped.[20]

Meanwhile, demands continued for the establishment of a biracial committee in Americus. Williams met regularly with local officials and businessmen seeking support for such a committee. At this point, he had several dozen SCOPE workers in Americus, including Iris, who participated in marches just about every day to exert pressure on the mayor to form a biracial committee. Local residents joined the SCOPE workers. At some of these protests, White onlookers threw beer bottles at the marchers, but most of the marches took place without trouble. Then, on August 4, the Sumter County attorney, at the urging of White business leaders, recommended to Mayor Walker that he go ahead and form a biracial committee. The mayor responded that he would only do so if all demonstrations and marches ceased immediately. Williams rejected this condition. Additionally, the mayor said he could not find any White residents willing to serve on any biracial committee because they feared for their businesses and lives. The goal of forming a biracial committee had failed once again.

On August 6, 1965, while Iris and her fellow SCOPE workers were still in Americus, President Johnson signed the federal Voting Rights Act (VRA) into law. In attendance at the White House signing ceremony were several civil rights leaders, including Martin Luther King Jr. As mentioned, passage of the act had been delayed for months due to filibusters led by senators from southern states, but now, at long last, the bill was finally the law of the land. Significantly, the VRA eliminated literacy tests, which had been a major barrier to Black registration in the South. On the night of August 6 in Americus, Iris and other supporters of civil rights celebrated passage of the VRA with a march to the courthouse and a rally at Friendship Baptist Church. Dick Gregory was in attendance and spoke to the crowd at the rally.

The next evening on August 7, Whites held a counter-rally in Americus to protest the VRA.[21] There the featured speaker was Lester Maddox, a segregationist politician making his way up the Georgia political ladder to an eventual governorship.[22] He was joined by hundreds of "concerned white citizens." As this rally played out, civil rights workers staged a countermarch nearby. The potential for violence existed, but police officers kept the two groups separated. On Sunday, August 8, fifteen hundred KKK members marched through the streets of Americus to the spot where Andrew Whatley had been shot and held a memorial service for him. City officials had asked the KKK not to hold the march or service, but when the KKK refused to change their plans, the officials asked the civil rights workers to remain in their homes during the march and service. Most, including Iris, complied with that request, and no confrontations between the KKK and SCOPE and SNCC workers and local Black residents occurred that day.

On August 9, Williams arranged for all SCOPE workers to leave Americus to attend the SCLC convention in Birmingham, Alabama. Racial tensions in Americus continued to simmer throughout the remainder of the summer of 1965. Picketing continued at White-owned stores that had no Black employees. The segregated churches still turned away Black worshippers. Police drove through Black neighborhoods and arrested residents for crimes such as jaywalking. Lawsuits were filed to stop police harassment. And countersuits were filed to end all marches. Still, in the city that Iris and her coworkers left behind, some progress had been made that summer. By the end of 1965, thirty-five hundred Black voters had been added to the voting rolls in Sumter County.

CHAPTER 6

Birmingham and Philadelphia

IRIS WAS GLAD THAT WILLIAMS had transferred her from Savannah to Americus. She now felt truly part of the civil rights movement. She believed that her participation in the marches and vigils in Americus had proved useful, unlike the time she had spent on the streets of Savannah. She had also heard John Lewis speak, and he had impressed her greatly. In short, her experience in Americus had made Iris feel that what she was doing was meaningful. She was determined to continue working for the movement. In Americus, Iris had spent more time with SNCC workers than SCOPE workers, especially after Boyd left for Atlanta. When Williams told the SCOPE workers that their time in Americus had ended, Iris considered staying there and joining SNCC. After some thought, however, she decided to go to the annual SCLC convention in Birmingham. It would be best for her to stick with her plans to work with SCOPE for the summer and return to Temple University for the fall semester. Still, it was with some sadness that Iris left Americus and boarded the bus to Birmingham for the SCLC annual meeting.

Once in Birmingham, Iris, like all SCOPE workers, was placed in the private home of a host family. Shortly after checking in with her host family, Iris and a group of other volunteers solemnly visited the church where, two years earlier, four young Black girls had been murdered. On September 15, 1963, Birmingham had experienced one of the most horrific acts of racist violence in United States history. Shortly before Sunday services were about to begin at the Sixteenth Street Baptist Church, a bomb that had been planted under the steps of the church exploded. The blast killed four girls and injured twenty other worshippers, including other children. The murders created outrage across the nation. Although the FBI's investigation identified four known KKK members as responsible for the bombing, no federal criminal charges were brought against the men. FBI Director Hoover claimed that any prosecutions would fail to succeed because of the unwillingness of any witnesses to testify and the lack of physical evidence. Many questioned Hoover's motives in his evaluation of the case. At the time of the SCLC annual convention, two years after the bombing, no one had yet been charged with the murders. Only many years later would criminal charges be brought and convictions obtained.[1] The church visit was another reminder to Iris of the very real racial hatred that led to violence against innocent people solely because of the color of their skin.

Later that day, Iris prepared for the annual meeting of the SCLC by reading some materials distributed to the SCOPE volunteers. SCLC was founded as a separate civil rights organization in 1957 at a meeting in Atlanta at the Ebenezer Baptist Church, where Martin Luther King Sr., "Daddy King," served as minister. About one hundred Black leaders, mostly ministers, agreed to form a new organization with a religious tilt and an emphasis on nonviolent direct action. Daddy King's son, Martin Luther King Jr., was selected as its first president. The purpose of the organization was to address the Jim Crow policies of the South with emphasis on bus desegregation, voter registration, and political education. The initial name of the organization was the Southern Leadership Conference on Transportation and Nonviolent Integration. This name was changed shortly thereafter to the Southern Christian Leadership Conference, which emphasized its connection to the church and the ministers involved in its formation. By the time of the 1965 annual meeting, SCLC had participated in major demonstrations in Albany, Georgia, and Birmingham and Selma, Alabama, as well as in the march to Montgomery, Alabama, and the March on Washington. SCLC also had been instrumental in the passage of the 1964 Civil Rights Act and the recently enacted Voting Rights Act. The 1965 SCLC annual meeting coincided with the ten-year anniversary of the Montgomery bus boycott, during which Rosa Parks became a hero for her courage in refusing to move out of the White section of a Montgomery public bus.[2] King Jr.'s role in the Montgomery bus boycott had thrust him into a position of leadership in the civil rights movement that he maintained the rest of his life.

Iris dutifully attended all the sessions at the annual meeting. There she heard many speeches of varying levels of interest to her. She best remembered Dr. King's presidential address.[3] In it, King gave special thanks to those students and local volunteers who had participated in that summer's SCOPE program. He noted that SCOPE was the largest voter registration drive in US history. Over 1,200 workers, including 650 college students, worked that summer in six southern states. The exact number of new voters registered by SCOPE was still unclear, but King was certain that SCOPE had been a success. He asked all SCOPE workers to stand. The crowd applauded as Iris and her fellow SCOPE workers stood and waved. Besides SCOPE and voter registration, King discussed SCLC's involvement with political education at "Citizenship Schools," and plans for economic boycotts as part of "Operation Breadbasket."[4]

Iris's most vivid memory of King's speech, however, was when he transitioned to discussing the Vietnam War,[5] an issue that also deeply concerned her. A few months prior to the SCLC annual meeting, King had urged President Johnson to negotiate with the National Liberation Front, also known as the Vietcong, to reach a peace agreement. King's position was based on several reasons. First, as a pacificist who based his opposition to all wars on his religious beliefs, King believed that "it is sinful for any of God's children to brutalize any of God's children." This position had been reinforced by his study of the writings of Mahatma Gandhi. King also saw the United States' prosecution of the Vietnam War as diverting resources from domestic needs such as education, job training, job creation, housing, health care, and poverty relief. In his speech at the SCLC annual meeting, King called for an immediate end to the bombing of North Vietnam, as well as for Hanoi to drop its demand that all US troops be withdrawn from South Vietnam before it would participate in any peace talks. At the end of his speech, King asked the audience to stand in support of all the programs and goals he had just discussed. Iris, along with most but not all of the others, stood and applauded.

As the partial standing ovation showed, the SCLC convention audience was not unanimous in its support for King's statements on

Vietnam. Indeed, the anti–Vietnam War stance articulated by King was not universally accepted by all members of the civil rights community. In August 1965, public opinion polls showed that 60 percent of all Americans supported the war effort and President Johnson's handling of it. Only 25 percent said that US military involvement in Vietnam was wrong. Most Black Americans supported the war, although at a slightly lower percentage than Whites.[6] The split among civil rights activists on this issue was based not as much on their opinion of the war itself as on the wisdom of devoting so many resources and energy to any cause other than civil rights for Black Americans. They also worried that some Whites who supported both the civil rights movement and the war effort might withdraw their support for those civil rights organizations that took an antiwar position. Initially, there was strong resistance within SCLC to King's antiwar view. By the time he made his comments at the organization's 1965 annual meeting, however, King had the support of most of the SCLC leadership.

Other civil rights organizations hesitated to take a public position on the Vietnam War. At its July 1965 convention, the Congress of Racial Equality (CORE) held a spirited debate on a motion to oppose United States involvement in Vietnam. The head of CORE, James Farmer, expressed his concern that adoption of an antiwar motion would damage support for CORE's civil rights agenda. The language of the motion also caused some concern. It not only called for the immediate withdrawal of all US troops but also condemned the war's "immoral policy of racism abroad." The convention ended up adopting an antiwar motion, but only a minority of the delegates in attendance actually voted in favor of it, with most delegates abstaining. Under the procedural rules previously adopted by CORE, the motion was considered adopted. One year later, however, at the 1966 convention, antiwar sentiment had grown, especially among CORE's student chapters, and a strong antiwar resolution passed easily.[7]

For its part, the National Association for the Advancement of Colored Persons (NAACP) declined to take a position against the Vietnam War during this time, preferring to focus on domestic civil rights issues. The Urban League, another civil rights organization, also viewed its role as limited to dealing with the horrors of Jim Crow and not the horrors of Vietnam. Again, it was not the case that these organizations supported the war effort, it's that they felt that it would detract from their effectiveness in achieving rights for Black Americans.[8]

On the other hand, SNCC from the beginning consistently and publicly opposed US involvement in the Vietnam War; it was the first mainstream civil rights organization to take such a public position.[9] SNCC based its opposition on several factors. First, because of its central tenet of nonviolence, they, like King, opposed all wars, not just the one in Vietnam. But SNCC opposition went beyond general adoption of pacificism. It spoke of the right of the Vietnamese people to self-determination. They also pointed out that it would be hypocritical for Black Americans arguing for their full rights in the United States to deny the right of the Vietnamese people to fight for self-determination in their own homeland. SNCC viewed US involvement in another nation's civil war as an example of a White superpower trying to suppress the rights of nonwhite people who sought to decide their own form of governance. They also based their anti–Vietnam War sentiment on the notion of anticolonialism. White Europeans had a long history of taking control of nonwhite societies on other continents for economic and political exploitation, of which the situation in Vietnam was just another example. Black men should not have to fight a war against other people of color at the behest of the American federal government. Why, SNCC leaders asked, should Black soldiers fight (and die) for democracy ten thousand miles away from their homes when democratic freedoms such as the right to vote were denied them in the United States? Moreover, casualties among Black combatants in Vietnam were disproportionate to the overall Black population in the United States.[10]

Along the same line of reasoning, SNCC saw the military draft as racist. Draft boards in the South, overwhelmingly composed of only Whites, drafted young Black men disproportionately to all those eligible for the draft.[11] Moreover, the deferment for college students, most of whom were White and from middle- and upper-class backgrounds, had a disproportionate impact on Black people in all areas of the country. Fewer Black males than White males attended college and were thereby eligible for this deferment. Additionally, even those Black men eligible for a student deferment, should they spend any time away from college to work for a civil rights organization, would have their student draft deferment taken away and soon find themselves drafted. SNCC saw this as evidence of the draft boards working to weaken the civil rights movement.

Some SNCC members who were drafted chose to leave the country or go to jail rather than fight in a war they did not support. One such person was Michael Simmons from Temple University, who had formed the group Conscience that Iris joined. It had been Simmons's commitment to civil rights that motivated Iris to take the next step in participating in the civil rights movement. Simmons left Temple University before graduating to work with SNCC, and he helped draft the official SNCC statement against the Vietnam War. Moreover, as part of SNCC's Atlanta Project, Simmons helped draft SNCC's "Black Consciousness" paper, which called for self-determination in the Black community and emphasized the importance of building Black-controlled institutions. He also served as a SNCC "campus traveler," working in Virginia, North Carolina, Georgia, Alabama, Mississippi, and Arkansas, and was arrested over ten times for his civil rights activities. Having left Temple University to actively participate on a full-time basis with SNCC, Simmons lost his college draft deferment. When he received his draft notification, he refused to be inducted, a decision for which he spent two and a half years in federal prison.[12] After serving his sentence, he returned to work with SNCC.

In January 1966 Julian Bond, also a SNCC member, was denied the Georgia state legislature seat to which he had been elected in November because of his support of SNCC's anti–Vietnam War stance. Bond did not take his rightful seat until a year later, following a unanimous US Supreme Court decision holding that Bond's rights under the First Amendment of the US Constitution had been violated by the Georgia legislature's refusal to seat him.[13] Bond found support not only from SNCC, but also from King and the SCLC. At the SCLC annual meeting in Birmingham, Iris recognized for the first time the interrelationship of the civil rights movement and the anti–Vietnam War movement. This made her even more committed to both movements.

When the SCLC annual meeting ended, all SCOPE workers were transported to Atlanta. From there, each SCOPE worker was driven back to the place where he or she first had been assigned for the summer. Before she was driven back to Savannah, however, Iris went to the Freedom House to see Boyd. Iris and Boyd had a happy reunion. He seemed to be doing well. When they parted, they agreed to stay in touch, but it would be many years before they saw each other again. By that time, both of their lives would have gone through many changes.

Iris returned to her host family in Savannah, but with only a couple more weeks left in that summer's SCOPE project, no voter registration activities were planned. The other SCOPE workers assigned to Savannah had already returned to their home colleges. Iris spent her remaining days in Savannah socializing with and thanking everyone she had met in her host family's neighborhood. She was amazed at how generous her hosts had been, even though they had so little.

Iris did not look forward to going back to Philadelphia. The new semester at Temple University would likely feel irrelevant after all she had just experienced that summer. She could not imagine how attending her college classes would have any impact on the inequality and injustice she had witnessed firsthand in the South. Her feelings were not uncommon among White middle-class students who became involved in the civil rights movement in the mid-1960s. Many of them felt a sense of guilt in leaving the local Black communities in which they had volunteered. The volunteer college students always knew that they had the option of leaving their posts and returning to a comfortable life any time they wanted, but that was not so with their southern Black hosts and their neighbors. Iris had never before felt privileged. Northeast Philadelphia was not a wealthy area, and very few of its residents had an education above the high school level. Just about everyone Iris's age was a first-generation college student. But compared to what she had experienced in Savannah and Americus, Northeast Philadelphia might as well have been Beverly Hills, California.

When it was finally time to leave Savannah, there were tearful goodbyes and promises to stay in touch and to visit, although everyone thought these promises would likely not be kept. Iris took a train from Savannah to Philadelphia. From the 30th Street Station, she called her mother Eva to let her know she was back in Philadelphia and planned to take the subway and a bus back to the house. Iris had to some extent kept in touch with her mother, though not with her father, during the summer. She had written to her mother once every two weeks or so, telling her that she was doing fine, eating properly, and getting along well with the others, who she described as nice people from colleges across the country. She never went into the specifics of her living arrangements or the dangers that she and the other SCOPE workers had faced. She also did not disclose that Boyd had been hospitalized after suffering a concussion from a violent assault by a Georgia State Police officer.

Iris was apprehensive upon her arrival home. Though her parents had angrily told her not to come back to their home if she joined SCOPE, this threat was not repeated in the letters that she received from Eva through her SCOPE mailing address. She did not think her parents would turn her away, but what happened when she knocked on the front door both surprised and upset her. Eva did not look excited or even pleased to see her. Morris did not even come to the door. Eva told Iris to leave her luggage outside the house, put its contents into large trash bags, and wash every item before putting anything into any closet or drawer of the house. This strongly reminded Iris of the policy of White-owned stores that forbade Black customers to try on clothes or return them, due to the racist belief that somehow Black people were "dirty," and by extension so was anything they touched.

When Iris finally entered the house, she said hello to her father, whose reaction was far from warm. Her parents made it clear that neither of them was pleased to see her back home. They told her that they did not want to hear anything about where she had been, what she had done, or with whom she had spent time. For the next couple weeks, Iris slept at her parents' house but barely spoke with them. She would spend the entire day visiting friends from high school and college until she came home at night. Eventually, she decided she could no longer stay with her parents. Without telling them that she was leaving or where she was going, she moved out. She waited until they had both left the house, and with the help of a friend moved her bed, some clothes, and other personal items to an apartment in the Powelton Village neighborhood of the city. A friend's roommate had moved out of the apartment, and Iris took her place. Powelton Village at the time was one of the few integrated areas of Philadelphia. Many students also lived there, as it was located between Temple University, the University of Pennsylvania, and Drexel University.

Iris began the fall 1965 semester at Temple as a social work major, thinking that due to her recent experiences, becoming a social worker would interest her. She applied for a loan for tuition through a federal student loan program and obtained a part-time job as a salesperson at a department store in downtown Philadelphia. She told her parents none of this. They made no effort to track her down, and she made no effort to contact them.

CHAPTER 7

Philadelphia and Washington, DC

WHEN SHE MOVED OUT of her parents' home to live at her friend's apartment, Iris went to the post office and completed a form to forward her mail to her new address. She was unsure if she would receive any mail from SCLC, but just in case, she did not want any mail delivered to her parents' house. Even if her parents knew where to find her, which at that point they did not, Iris doubted that they would forward her mail, especially any letters from SCLC. One of the first forwarded pieces of mail Iris received was a questionnaire from SCLC asking about her summer experience with SCOPE.[1] It was a one-page form with six questions, and about 1.5 inches of space provided for each answer:

1. What personal value do you think you received from participation in the summer project?
2. What contribution do you feel your SCOPE unit made to the community?
3. What serious problems, doubts, or questions have been raised in your mind as a result of your work this summer?
4. What suggestions would you have for future summer projects?
5. In what way will your experiences this summer affect your future?
6. In what way has your participation in SCOPE changed your outlook on life?

Iris decided that she did not want to write any answers in the spaces provided. She did not want to criticize the program or anyone involved, but she felt that were she to complete the form, she would need to answer each question honestly. The best solution, therefore, was not to return the form. Her honest answers, which she could not have articulated in the tiny spaces provided anyway, would reveal that she had found the program disorganized; that the orientation had inadequately prepared her for her time in Savannah; that the orientation should have focused more on training than on motivation; that Hosea Williams was not very nice to her (or anyone else); and that she felt that her time in Savannah had accomplished very little. On the other hand, her time in Americus had been positive, and she was happy that she had been able to participate in numerous marches and demonstrations there. Additionally, if Iris had completed the form, she would have written that for the first time in her life, she had personally witnessed extreme poverty and overt racism. White southerners' hatred of and violence against Black residents and civil rights workers of all races had upset her greatly. At the same time, she had met incredibly wonderful people. Her host families had virtually nothing, but were nonetheless willing to share everything. Her fellow SCOPE workers and the SNCC workers she encountered in Americus were extremely sincere in working for a better world. Yes, she was frustrated and disappointed in what she had personally been able to accomplish, but she was not going to give up. She had changed her major to social work, which she hoped would be useful in bringing about the changes so desperately needed. She hoped to become involved in another project to help the civil rights movement. At this point, however, it was unclear to her what would be her next such step in the movement.

Within SCLC, there was a discussion of SCOPE's future. At an SCLC executive staff meeting held at the end of August, Williams gave a report on the SCOPE project.[2] Among those attending this meeting were Dr. King, Andrew Young, James Bevel, Stanley Levison, James Orange, and Walter E. Fauntroy. Williams stated that the "most important" result of SCOPE was that "so many Negroes have been aroused and motivated." He reported that the project had cost SCLC about $165,000, and suggested that SCOPE continue in summer 1966 in the same locations to get the "full benefit from the investment already made." He thought that with the newly registered voters, it was "now possible to elect Negro public officials in many communities and that the project's ultimate goal is to remove racism" from politics. SCOPE had provided experience to many "dedicated persons" to "learn the art of running for public office." Williams's report was followed by a discussion among the group on the need to determine how to "get the best results for the resources allocated." It was pointed out that some benefits of SCOPE, such as "the willingness of white people to come [to the South] and work and the inspiration afforded in communities across the South by their very presence," were not easily quantified. It was also discussed that the name SCOPE was a "barrier," and should be changed to Voter Registration and Education Project.

Not all SCLC officials were impressed by SCOPE. On August 25, 1965, Randolph Blackwell, an executive staff member, wrote a "confidential memorandum" to Dr. King and Rev. Ralph Abernathy. After stating that some people had seen SCOPE as the vehicle for SCLC to build a grassroots movement, he wanted to "be clear and precise. The SCOPE project as it presently exists should be brought to end just as soon as it possibly can without inviting public inquiry." He continued: "In my candid opinion, the project has degenerated in the main to an experiment in liquor and sex, compounded by criminal conduct," including suspected rapes. Blackwell also accused SCOPE of "financial dishonesty," "the most dangerous kind of irresponsible quest for publicity," and "has placed in question the whole matter of how serious can twentieth-century western civilization be about human dignity because of the fact that SCLC is a leader in this great cause."[3] When I showed this memorandum to Iris years later, she laughed, and told me that this did not describe the SCOPE in which she participated. There had always been rumors that college students volunteered for civil rights work so that they could engage in unlimited sex, especially interracial sex. Iris assured me that she knew no one, including herself, who had joined SCOPE for reasons other than the advancement of the civil rights movement. I told her of what Stokely Carmichael had written in his autobiography on this point: If any White woman was interested in having sex with Black men, he would clearly recommend traveling to Jamaica over doing civil rights work in the South.[4] It should be noted that Blackwell and Williams often disagreed over SCLC policy, and that everyone recognized the personal conflicts between them. These tensions led Blackwell to leave SCLC leadership in 1966.[5]

In November 1965, as a follow-up to his oral report at the August executive staff meeting, Williams wrote a memorandum to Dr. King and the SCLC board of directors reviewing SCOPE's 1965 summer program.[6] Over twelve hundred people took part in the summer program. Six hundred and fifty college students participated, representing about one hundred and twenty colleges and universities. Four hundred local volunteers also participated. Approximately seventy thousand Black people had tried to register to vote in the areas served by SCOPE, and approximately forty-nine thousand succeeded in doing so. To add context to these numbers, in the areas in which SCOPE had worked, there were about one million Black residents, of whom about three hundred thousand were now registered. Williams wrote that "comparing the number of dollars spent with the number of Negroes registered would be distorting the facts."[7] This comment was made in response to criticism that SCOPE had been too costly. Rather, Williams continued in his memorandum, one needed to evaluate SCOPE based on its "bringing so many white persons into the movement from varied elevations of life" for the first time. Moreover, "thousands of Negroes across the Southland were able to witness their first sincere, dedicated white person in their quest for equality."[8] He also noted that about a hundred SCOPE workers had decided not to return to college at the summer's end so that they could continue to work for SCLC.

After having read the evaluation forms that were returned by the past summer's SCOPE workers, Williams addressed some of the concerns that had been expressed in them. He acknowledged that some SCOPE workers complained of lack of organization, remarking that in his opinion, flexibility did not equal disorganization: "You've got to know how to respond to the situation, almost abruptly, instantly." The SCOPE "kids" did not realize that "you can't organize a movement."[9] Moreover, Williams noted, "some of the kids were even kind of frustrated, they thought they'd be able to free the Negro this summer, bring freedom to America this summer." Even though the White college student SCOPE workers were "green," he wrote, they were "probably the finest group of volunteers of non-Southerners that has ever been assembled by the civil rights movement. You know, none of the goof-offs and mess-ups, and persons with ill-will intentions. So we ended up with a fine group of people, the most dedicated, the most idealistic concerned group of non-Southerners ever assembled for any civil rights project, movement project."[10]

Williams's report discussed how SCOPE had a big impact on both northern White and southern Black volunteers. "You can't look on the television and hear radio and understand and comprehend the scope of a situation. So for these kids to come down here, now they know how vicious segregation is, they know what a miserable life Black people have to live, how fearful you have to be. A lot of these kids realize for the first time in their lives what a terrible predicament, what a hell of a shape, America is in." Regarding Black southerners, Williams commented that because of SCOPE,

> Negroes in many of the black-belt counties for the first time in their lives were able to meet, to eat with, to talk with, to work with decent white people, white people that were sincere, white people that were attempting at least to understand their problem, white people that felt like the Negroes' problem was their problem, white people that did not look down upon them like they were grime or dirt or slaves, white people that want to help them realize their dignity and realize they're somebody though they may be poor. This is a revelation. In many of these counties, this is the first time in the history of the Negro that white people had slept in the homes of black people.[11]

Williams's plan was to continue the SCOPE program the following summer with expansion into more counties and more emphasis on political education. His plan never came to fruition, however, for as it turned out, SCOPE existed for only one summer, the summer of 1965.

During the fall of 1965, Iris was busy working in a retail store and attending classes at Temple University. She decided that she should cut back temporarily from civil rights activism, and therefore did not get involved in any organizations on campus or in the city. For now, she needed to focus on making enough money to pay her tuition and support herself. She did not see her parents. Although she formally switched her major to social work, in which she did have an interest, Iris found most of her classes boring and irrelevant to what she wanted to accomplish. She had hoped, like so many of the "green" SCOPE workers of which Williams spoke, to make a real difference, but for now, she was just trying to get back to the life of a college student.

Things changed, however, at the end of the fall semester. Ever since Iris heard Dr. King speak about Vietnam at the SCLC annual meeting in Birmingham, she'd thought about the connection between the civil rights movement and the anti–Vietnam War movement. The weekend before Thanksgiving, she saw a flyer posted on a classroom wall that gave notice of the March on Washington for Peace in Vietnam, scheduled for Saturday, November 27, two days after Thanksgiving. After unsuccessfully trying to convince others to go with her to the march, she decided to go by herself. That Saturday, Iris took an early bus from Philadelphia to Washington, DC, arriving about 10:00 a.m. She intended to take a bus back home in the evening after the rally. Upon her arrival in Washington, Iris followed a crowd of mostly young college and high-school-aged people that appeared to know where to go. The crowd brought her to the White House. Most everyone assembled was quite peaceful and generally quiet. Some, though not many, held signs. Iris later learned that the organizers of the march had "authorized" certain slogans on signs, such as "Stop the Bombing," but had discouraged messages such as "End the Draft." Also discouraged was the waving of Vietcong flags.[12] Originally, the organizers of the event had decided to totally ban the participation of any person carrying an unauthorized sign that others might view as "too radical." They eventually decided, however, that it would be better to "ignore" such signs and simply request that participants not display them.

Crowd estimates varied. The police figured that between fifteen and twenty-five thousand people attended the march, whereas the organizers put the crowd at around fifty thousand.[13] Whatever the actual count, newspaper accounts reported that the march was an "orderly and strangely silent" protest for peace in Vietnam. They described the marchers as mostly "mild mannered," "surprisingly neat," and "of high caliber."[14] The march around the White House lasted from about 11:00 a.m. to 1:00 p.m. President Johnson was at his Texas ranch that day, not at the White House. Across Pennsylvania Avenue in Lafayette Park, an estimated one thousand to fifteen hundred counterdemonstrators had gathered, holding signs such as "Bomb Hanoi" and "Dodgers only win ball games."[15] Among the counterdemonstrators were members of the American Nazi Party, including its leader, George Lincoln Rockwell. A fight broke out between Nazi Party members and peace marchers when Rockwell tried to grab a Vietcong flag. Several people on both sides were arrested for disorderly conduct, including Rockwell.[16] Still, in general, the atmosphere was overwhelmingly peaceful.

As Iris marched around the White House as part of the protest, she did not recognize anyone she knew. At about 1:00 p.m., she followed the crowd to the National Mall and joined them in sitting on the grass around the Washington Monument. It was a beautiful fall day, with sunny skies and temperatures in the upper sixties. About 2:00 p.m., the speeches began. By this point, Iris sat among a group of about twenty-five people, both male and female, Black and White. During the speeches the members of this group, including Iris, began to interact with one another.

The March on Washington for Peace in Vietnam was viewed (and criticized by some) as a "moderate" rebuke of Johnson's Vietnam War policy. The organizers supported a negotiated settlement of the conflict, not a unilateral withdrawal of US forces from Vietnam. It was billed not as a protest march but one meant to promote what were called "positive proposals." The goals included a negotiated ceasefire, the end of all bombing of North Vietnam, no more American troops and weapons sent to Vietnam, and United Nations involvement in talks to end the war. No one called for civil disobedience or draft resistance. The tone of the speeches was moderate, not inflammatory. This perhaps can be understood because at the time of the march "only" one thousand American soldiers had been killed in Vietnam. As the number of American deaths increased dramatically, along with Vietnamese deaths, the antiwar protests in later years became more intense.

The coordinator of the 1965 march was Sanford Gottlieb.[17] Since 1960, he had been the political action director for the National Committee for a Sane Nuclear Policy, known as SANE. SANE was founded in 1957 to gain support for a nuclear test ban treaty. When such a treaty was adopted, SANE broadened its goal to achieve worldwide disarmament. Gottlieb had also been one of the leaders of the 1963 March on Washington. For the 1965 protest, Gottlieb had arranged an impressive group of activists from both the civil rights and antiwar movements to speak. For Iris, the speakers once again tied both movements together. Many years later, she recalled the "riveting speech" by SCLC's Bayard Rustin. Rustin had been involved in the civil rights movement since the 1940s and a close adviser to King since the Montgomery bus boycott. He was one of the leaders of the Freedom Rides in 1961 and the March on Washington in 1963. His role with SCLC was somewhat controversial, however, because he had also been a member of the Communist Party USA, and was openly gay. Some of King's other advisers cautioned King that Rustin's past political affiliation and his sexual orientation would damage the civil rights movement. Later in his life, Rustin took positions contrary to those of most other civil rights leaders. For example, he opposed racial programs calling for reparations for African Americans and argued against affirmative action in employment and college admissions. He also rejected his earlier pacificist views and became a strong anti-Communist who supported military intervention to defeat the spread of "international Communism." At the time of his speech in 1965, however, Rustin passionately expressed his opposition to US involvement in the Vietnam War.

Another who spoke that day from the civil rights movement was Coretta Scott King, Dr. King's wife.[18] Iris was pleased to hear a woman speak at the rally. At this time, women were underrepresented in leadership roles in both the civil rights and antiwar movements. Another speaker who Iris recalled hearing was Dr. Benjamin Spock, who at the time was known more for his child-raising theories than his political views. Over the next few years, however, Spock became a well-known antiwar activist. In 1972, he was the People's Party nominee for president of the United States, running on the platform of ending US involvement in the Vietnam War.

Carl Ogelsby, the president of Students for a Democratic Society (SDS), also spoke. Iris had attended a few SDS meetings at Temple but never joined. After hearing Ogelsby's remarks, however, she decided to reconsider the SDS when she got back to Philadelphia. Iris also found the antiwar comments presented by Norman Thomas, leader of the Socialist Party of the United States, very intriguing, although she was not yet philosophically ready to join that organization. She also remembered seeing Ossie Davis and Ruby Dee, both from the entertainment industry, at the podium in support of ending US involvement in Vietnam. Actor Tony Randall also took the stage at the rally, as did John Lewis of SNCC and James Farmer of CORE. *Fahrenheit 451* author Ray Bradbury; Nobel Prize for Literature winner Saul Bellow;

John Hersey, author of the Pulitzer Prize–winning nonfiction book *Hiroshima*; social psychologist Erich Fromm; Michael Harrington, author of *The Other America*, who Iris had heard speak at the SCOPE orientation; cartoonist Jules Feiffer; medical researcher Dr. Albert Sabin, who developed the oral polio vaccine; artist Alexander Calder; and playwright Arthur Miller, most famous for *Death of a Salesman*, were all present. What a group! All of them spoke out against the war! Iris was overwhelmed to be at the same rally in such distinguished company.

Most significantly, Iris was excited to be among other like-minded people, not only the estimated fifteen to fifty thousand people at the rally on the National Mall but especially the small group of people with whom she sat. These people started out as total strangers who just so happened to sit in the same area, but during the rally they introduced themselves, shared drinks and food, and discussed the anti–Vietnam War and civil rights movements. Over their couple of hours together, they realized they shared many of the same values. Iris, at nineteen, appeared to be the youngest of the group, which ranged in age up to about fifty years old. When the speeches ended and the crowd began to disperse, the people around Iris made no effort to leave. Their discussions continued, covering such topics as how the war might be ended, what approaches the civil rights movement should take, the role of women in both movements, and whether it was better to work within or outside the present political structure. These discussions continued until it began to get dark, and still, no one wanted to leave. One of the White men, seemingly the oldest among the group, invited the others to his home in the Georgetown section of the city, where they could continue their discussions. All agreed to reconvene at his house about an hour later. Iris walked to the Georgetown address with a few others. Among those with whom she walked was Curtis Styles. As they walked together, Iris told Curtis that she had spent the summer with the SCLC/SCOPE project in Savannah and Americus, Georgia, and she currently studied Social Work at Temple University. In turn, Curtis told Iris of his background.

Curtis was a twenty-six-year-old Black man from Mississippi.[19] As a high school student, he had been active in the movement to integrate the Biloxi public beaches. When Black people, including Curtis, tried to swim at a Whites-only beach, rioting broke out. After graduating high school in Biloxi, Curtis attended Southern University in Baton Rouge, Louisiana, a HBCU (historically Black college or university), where he continued his civil rights activism and joined SNCC. Since graduation, Curtis had worked full time for SNCC in Hattiesburg, Mississippi. At the time of the 1965 antiwar march, he was a SNCC project director in Columbia, Mississippi, a small town about thirty miles west of Hattiesburg. He had been on his way to Detroit to pick up a car donated by a SNCC supporter when he decided to take a detour to Washington, DC, to attend the antiwar rally. He planned to leave Washington for Detroit on the Sunday after Thanksgiving by bus and then drive the car from Detroit to Columbia, where Curtis lived in a small house with two other SNCC workers, a White man, Ira Grupper, and W. J. McClenton, who was Black. The three men worked tirelessly on various SNCC initiatives in this small Mississippi town, and they and other SNCC workers would use the car.

Iris and Curtis met up with the others at the Georgetown house. Although Iris had no recollection of the homeowner's name or the name of the street on which the house was located, she did remember that it was a large house, beautifully decorated, and obviously expensive. The owner must have been very wealthy. As soon as everyone from the group arrived, the political discussions began again. At one point, the owner of the house suggested that he might consider funding a new organization focused on issues involving racism and world peace, an offer that was greeted with applause. Nothing more was said about this hypothetical new organization, but the group talked throughout the night and into the early morning, when the owner's private cook served breakfast and coffee to those who remained.

All through the night, Iris sat next to Curtis. He was more vocal in his opinions, but Iris also actively participated in the conversation, and felt no sexism among the group when she expressed her opinions. This seemed to her to be a very egalitarian group whose goal was to try to solve all the problems in the nation, and indeed the world. By late morning everyone was exhausted, both mentally and physically. No concrete plans had been made, but everyone agreed that it had been a wonderful experience, and that they should all stay in touch and get together again. That never happened.

As everyone in the group was leaving, Curtis asked Iris whether she would be interested in traveling to Detroit with him to pick up the donated car. He said he would pay for her bus ticket to Detroit and then take her back to Philadelphia before driving the donated car to Mississippi.

"Are you interested in coming with me?" Curtis asked.

"Yes. Great," Iris responded. "Sounds like fun."

CHAPTER 8

Detroit to Columbia

IRIS AND CURTIS TOOK A taxicab to the bus station and boarded a bus to Detroit. Although she had never expected things to develop as they did, she was prepared to go to Detroit for the night: She had packed a small bag with some clothes and toiletries before going to Washington, DC, just in case the rally ended too late to take a bus back to Philadelphia that Saturday night. They both got some sleep on the bus, but when they were awake, they continued their discussion of the civil rights movement and the plight of Black people in the South. Iris shared her experiences from SCOPE, especially her time in Americus. She told Curtis about the other SNCC workers she had met there, and the time she heard John Lewis speak. She also told him that she had been impressed by how well organized SNCC was. Curtis told Iris that he was glad to hear that she had a positive view of SNCC. He had worked for the organization for several years and recruited many other workers. He asked Iris if she was interested in learning more about the group. When Iris said she was extremely interested, Curtis started from the beginning.

In 1960 in Greensboro, North Carolina, he told Iris, students began a sit-in movement against segregated lunch counters. These protests, often held at a Woolworth's variety store that had a lunch counter, were nonviolent. Indeed, nonviolence was a key element to the early protests, even though the protesters were often harassed and sometimes physically attacked by white bystanders and store workers. Many of the early protesters attended HBCUs and divinity schools. In April 1960 Ella Baker, at the time the executive director of SCLC, organized a convention at Shaw University in Raleigh, North Carolina, an HBCU that Baker had attended. Baker was not satisfied with existing civil rights organizations like SCLC, NAACP, and CORE; she wanted to create a different kind of organization, one that would encourage young people to get involved with the civil rights movement.[1] Over two hundred people, mostly college students, attended this convention, among them Marion Barry, James Bevel, Julian Bond, Stokely Carmichael, Bernard LaFayette, James Lawson, John Lewis, and Diane Nash, all of whom went on to become prominent leaders in the civil rights movement. Marion Barry, a graduate student at the HBCU Fisk University who later served as mayor of Washington, DC, was elected as SNCC's first chairperson.

Baker also envisioned the new organization as one led by Black people. Although SNCC included some White members, it was not formed as an interracial organization per se. Whites did not serve in any leadership roles; White workers followed direction from Black leaders. That said, not all SNCC members rejected the concept of an interracial civil rights movement. Curtis told Iris that he was among those who welcomed white members; his recruiting was multi-racial. He did say, however, that SNCC's focus was to have Black people in control to strengthen local Black participation, and not to have to rely on "liberal Whites." He admitted to Iris that the role of Whites within SNCC was a constant source of tension among its members.

Within one year of its formation, SNCC had gained support from activists of other organizations who found SNCC's tenets attractive. For example, SNCC was at the forefront of the "Jail, No Bail" policy, which called on civil rights workers jailed for their activism to refuse to post bail, instead remaining in jail to draw public attention to the justness of their cause and the unfairness of their arrests. Dr. King and SCLC adopted this policy. Iris commented that when she was in Americus, the four Black women arrested for trying to vote in a Whites-only line had remained in jail even when local White businessmen offered to pay their bail. SNCC also found wide support for its insistence on nonviolent protest and its sponsorship of training sessions on nonviolent tactics. These sessions included role-playing by SNCC members as both White racists and Black victims. James Lawson of SNCC was well known for the nonviolence training he offered to college students in Nashville.

SNCC had played a leading role in the Freedom Rides of the spring of 1961, staged in response to *Boynton v. Virginia*,[2] a Supreme Court case decided in December 1960 in which the court held that segregated terminals for interstate bus and train riders were illegal. The original plan for the Freedom Rides was spearheaded by CORE. To test enforcement of the *Boynton* decision, the organization arranged for volunteers to board buses in Washington, DC, headed for New Orleans. This bus trip would take the riders through Virginia, Alabama, Mississippi, and Louisiana. The volunteer Freedom Riders encountered no significant problems until they reached Alabama, where White racists set a bus on fire and attacked the riders, beating them as they fled from the burning vehicle. At this point, CORE decided to cancel the Freedom Rides lest one of the protesters lose their lives. When CORE tried to pull the plug, SNCC decided to take control. The bus trip continued to New Orleans via Birmingham, Alabama, with about twenty new volunteers, mostly college students from SNCC's Nashville affiliate. Ignoring CORE's warnings not to go, they were determined to finish the ride. When these "reinforcement" riders arrived in Birmingham, some were immediately arrested, some were beaten by members of the KKK, and others suffered "only" verbal abuse. Those not arrested or injured vowed to continue the trip. The next stop was Jackson, Mississippi, where the riders were arrested upon arrival and put in jail. The jailed Freedom Riders, following the "Jail, No Bail" policy, refused to allow anyone to post bail for them, even though they received many offers. When more reinforcement riders arrived in Jackson, they too were jailed. At one point, over three hundred Freedom Riders were held in Jackson jails. As this was well above the capacity of the local jails, Mississippi officials transferred the jailed Freedom Riders to Parchman Farm, a facility with a well-deserved reputation as one of the worst prisons in the entire country.[3] Most of those arrested were released within a few days, but some were held for several months. SNCC was instrumental in keeping the Freedom Rides going by recruiting new volunteers, supporting hunger strikes, and organizing demonstrations. None of their white attackers was ever punished.

Curtis explained to Iris that he had wanted to join the Freedom Rides but was told to stay in Biloxi with the segregated beach project. Although Iris had heard of the Freedom Rides before, Curtis's description of them made the protest much more meaningful and personal to her. Curtis also noted that SNCC, as opposed to other civil rights organizations, tended to focus on the "tougher" places.[4] Iris told him that she could not imagine places much worse than Americus, Georgia, where she had worked with SCLC and SCOPE. His response was that conditions in Mississippi made other parts of the South seem tame. He told her about Mississippi's infamous White Citizens' Councils, private vigilante groups that terrorized Black people. Then there was the Mississippi Sovereignty Commission, an official Mississippi state government agency that harassed and spied on civil rights workers, created by the Mississippi legislature in 1956 in response to the 1954 Supreme Court ruling in *Brown v. Board of Education*,[5] which declared unconstitutional the long-standing separate but equal doctrine in public school education. The express statutory purpose of the Sovereignty Commission was to preserve and protect segregation by "protecting" Mississippi citizens from federal enforcement of *Brown* and other federal civil rights laws and Supreme Court rulings.[6] The commission compiled lists of people suspected of involvement in civil rights work, and Curtis was certain he and his fellow SNCC co-workers were on the list. In any event, by keeping tabs on people on the list, the commission could alert local police and private vigilante groups such as the White Citizens' Councils and the KKK to planned civil rights meetings, marches, boycotts, and voter registration drives. This official state agency not only tolerated illegal police harassment but encouraged and supported it. The Sovereignty Commission also engaged in media campaigns with local newspapers and radio and television outlets to spread disinformation. It called civil rights workers "outside agitators," claimed they were Communists, and described them in military terms, using words such as *invaders* and *terrorists*. It also called them degenerates and debauchers, promoting a popular rumor that northern civil rights workers came down to Mississippi to engage in unlimited sex with members of both races.[7]

Civil rights workers also had to contend with the Mississippi State Police and local police forces. County officials authorized spending to buy their police departments military troop carriers, mounted searchlights, horses, dogs, and personnel trailers for making mass arrests. The FBI also targeted civil rights groups including SNCC through its COINTELPRO operation.[8] Some SNCC volunteers were suspected of being FBI informants. All these groups made life in Mississippi dangerous for anyone promoting racial equality. Curtis gave Iris a couple examples: SNCC worker Bob Moses, he told her, had been arrested and jailed for trying to register Black people. He spent two days in jail before being released without any charges filed. Upon his release, however, he was attacked by a member of a local White Citizens' Council. Surprisingly, the white man who beat Moses was arrested and put on trial. Unsurprisingly, an all-White jury acquitted the man. Another SNCC worker, Bob Zellner, was beaten in McComb, Mississippi, in 1961.[9] No one was convicted of the attack on Zellner. Iris told Curtis that she had heard about this because her co-worker in SCOPE, Boyd Faust, was from McComb. And then there was Herbert Lee, a Black man who worked with SNCC, who was killed in Mississippi.[10] Lee's murder was witnessed by another Black man who identified the killer. The accused murderer was a member of the Mississippi State House of Representatives. After the witness came forward to identify the killer, he was severely beaten for giving his testimony. Not only were no charges filed against Lee's murderer, but a couple years later the witness too was murdered—yet another crime that went unpunished. Iris took in all of this in disbelief. She asked if Columbia, where Curtis lived currently, was this bad. He replied probably not, but who knew what could happen anywhere in Mississippi.

As the bus neared Detroit, Curtis continued to tell Iris more about SNCC's involvement in civil rights activities. In 1963 the group organized a mock "Freedom Vote" designed to show that the low rate of Black voter registration was due not to a lack of interest in voting among eligible Black voters but to roadblocks put up by racist Whites that made voting difficult, if not impossible for Black people.[11] In 1962, statistics indicated, only 6.2 percent of eligible Black Mississippians were registered to vote. The local White response was that Black people were not interested in voting. The SNCC mock election unmasked this falsehood. The rate of Black voter registration stayed low due to barriers such as the civics test questions that Black people were required to answer. For example, Mississippi voting registrars required Black people to answer questions related to any of the two hundred and eighty-five sections of the Mississippi Constitution. Moreover, whether an answer given was acceptable lay within the sole discretion of the county registrar—and in Mississippi, you can bet that all registrars were White. At the same time, White voters taking the qualifying test miraculously never flunked.

SNCC's mock elections first involved mock voter registration. Election sites were set up in churches and Black businesses. Then those "registered" voted for candidates for the political positions of governor and lieutenant governor. The project was successful in that approximately eighty thousand Black people registered and voted. This demonstrated that Black people were indeed interested in participating in the electoral process if given the opportunity to do so.

SNCC was also involved with the 1964 Freedom Summer. Curtis explained that SNCC was part of a coalition of civil rights groups that came together to form the Council of Federated Organizations (COFO). Although COFO included SCLC, NAACP, and CORE, SNCC played the largest role in the umbrella organization. Bob Moses was a SNCC field director who served as vice president of COFO and directed Freedom Summer.

COFO's plan was to register Black voters in Mississippi and run "Freedom Schools" to provide political education. Interviews were held on college campuses for volunteers. One question asked of the White college student applicants was whether they would have a problem working under the direction of a Black leader. Anyone who indicated any hesitation on this point was rejected. Moreover, any applicant who mentioned any interest in interracial dating was rejected. In June 1964 a training conference was held at Miami University in Oxford, Ohio, attended by about three hundred college students. The majority of them were White and from northern and western colleges. The average family income of the White volunteers was 50 percent above the national median. About 40 percent of the total group were women, and Curtis mentioned to Iris that many of them were Jewish. At the training, the student volunteers learned about race relations in Mississippi and the danger of trying to get Black people to register to vote there. In fact, that summer, eighty Freedom Summer workers had been beaten, four had been killed, and four had been critically wounded. Additionally, in those areas into which Freedom Workers were sent, thirty-seven Black churches and thirty Black-owned businesses or homes had been burned or bombed. Iris told Curtis that she was familiar with Freedom Summer and the tragic deaths of three civil rights workers in Philadelphia, Mississippi. Her parents had used these murders as a reason for opposing her involvement in SCOPE.

SNCC had also been instrumental in Selma, Alabama. Iris told Curtis that she had worked closely with Hosea Williams in Savannah and that he had told her of his leadership role in Selma. Curtis agreed that SCLC and Williams had played an important role in Selma, but he added that in his opinion SNCC had played a more significant role. Curtis explained how SNCC had spent years in Selma, working with local residents to organize voter registration drives, long before Dr. King and SCLC arrived there. This complaint was familiar to Iris, who had heard SNCC workers in Americus grumble that SCLC had just "showed up" in Selma to take credit for the good work done by SNCC.[12] Curtis told her how disappointed he and others in SNCC had been when, on the second attempt to cross the Edmund Pettis Bridge, King and other SCLC officials turned around and called off the march rather than confront the police. He thought that, in general, the national news media had given too much credit to SCLC and not enough to SNCC. He also reminded Iris that, just as in Selma, SNCC had been working in Americus for several years on voter registration before SCLC got involved.

Finally, Curtis discussed how SNCC operated and how it differed from other civil rights organizations. SNCC focused on building grassroots community organizations led by the local residents themselves, and it was more concerned with issues faced by those at the lower end of the economic hierarchy, such as sharecroppers, laborers, and female domestic workers, than those issues of concern to Black elites. SNCC workers viewed themselves not as leaders of the communities they tried to assist but as community organizers working to empower local people to take control. SNCC tended to work in small rural towns rather than urban areas, which was one reason why it did not receive the same amount of media attention as other organizations. There was also a difference between the different civil rights groups' level of involvement in the established political structure: SCLC favored working with political leaders in Washington, DC, lobbying for legislation such as the 1964 Civil Rights Act and the 1965 Voting Rights Act, whereas SNCC saw less value in federal legislation because it did not trust the federal government to enforce the laws. Consequently, SNCC did not engage in legislative lobbying. Additionally, SCLC was anxious to form an alliance with the Democratic Party, while SNCC still distrusted the Democratic Party after its treatment of the Mississippi Freedom Democratic Party at the 1964 Atlantic City nominating convention. Additionally, unlike the NAACP, SNCC did not engage in litigation. Although the NAACP Legal Defense Fund had been a successful force in the civil rights battle, SNCC did not rely on court cases to achieve change. Curtis also explained that SNCC's position on racial integration was different. SNCC was not as much focused on achieving integration as it was on seeking structural changes in society itself, especially fighting systemic racism.

Iris listened carefully as Curtis gave his presentation on SNCC. He cautioned that some of his statements were, naturally, just his opinions, and that it was impossible to fully explain complex organizations such as SNCC or SCLC during a bus ride. He asked if Iris had any questions or thoughts. She replied that after hearing him talk about SNCC, she hoped she could find a position with it the following summer. Maybe he could help her. Did he know of any SNCC programs that might be able to use her? It was at this point that Curtis asked Iris, "Why wait until next summer? How about coming to Columbia now?" Although this caught Iris off-guard, she found herself replying, "Sounds good. Yes."

Iris's quick acceptance of his not-well-thought-out offer gave Curtis pause. Realizing that maybe he had done too good of a job selling SNCC, he said, "I'm glad you are interested, but I really didn't expect you to say yes, so I think we need to discuss this further." He wanted to make sure Iris knew precisely what to expect. With some time still left until their bus arrived in Detroit, he began to tell Iris what she would encounter in Columbia.

If she came to Columbia, Curtis said, she should not expect immediate success. If she was looking for quick results and gratification, Columbia was not for her. Progress was slow and measured in multiples of years, not months or weeks. Moreover, the housing situation in Columbia was not ideal. Did she mind sleeping on the floor on a stained mattress that many others had used? Did she mind sleeping in one room with three men? It could also be dangerous. Even libraries were attacked! Curtis told her about the bombing of a SNCC-operated library that had been destroyed in Laurel.

He continued with more war stories,[13] warning her that not everyone who goes to Mississippi comes back uninjured—or alive. Was Iris willing to put herself in this position? It was important to Curtis that Iris was not signing up for the wrong reasons. All civil rights organizations had similar rules: No college students who were flunking out and looking for a good excuse to avoid school. No kids in rebellion, looking to get back at their parents. No martyrs looking for redemption through personal suffering. No beatniks, flakes, druggies, or mystics. The prospective volunteer needed to have the discipline to not lose control, retaliate, or become violent when subjected to verbal and physical abuse. Anyone who saw going to jail as a badge of honor or courage would be rejected, as would anyone who viewed going to jail as proof of their commitment to the civil rights movement or of official membership in the movement.[14] Iris raised several red flags in Curtis's mind. She had told him briefly about her parents' opposition to her involvement with SCOPE. Naturally, he wondered: Did she wish to join SNCC to get back at her parents? Iris also had mentioned how boring she found her classes. Was she looking for an excuse to quit college? Finally, while Iris seemed "normal" to Curtis, here he was talking to a nineteen-year-old White woman he had just met one day before who had traveled by herself to an anti–Vietnam War rally in Washington. Now, on a bus to Detroit, she'd just announced that she wanted to move to Columbia, Mississippi, where she would live with him and two other men about whom she knew practically nothing. This was not normal. Was she hiding anything? Was something wrong with her? It crossed Curtis's mind that maybe Iris had a sexual interest in him, which might have something to do with her willingness to go to Columbia. Were that the case, she would not have been the first White college female looking for a sexual fling with him. But any doubts Curtis may have harbored concerning Iris were misplaced, he soon realized. The true reason for her interest in Curtis, Columbia, and SNCC was her strong desire to become a serious worker with the civil rights movement. After talking more with her, Curtis concluded that she was indeed sincere about working with SNCC in Columbia—and doing so for the right reasons. If she insisted on going to Mississippi with him, he wouldn't stop her.

At the bus station in Detroit, another SNCC worker met them with the donated car. Because Curtis and Iris had gotten only a few hours' sleep on the bus, everyone agreed it would be best for the two of them to stay at the home of Curtis's friend before leaving Detroit. That night, Iris told Curtis that she had thought more about what she should do, and she had made her final decision: She would go to Columbia with him. A problem existed, however, in that she had only brought clothes for one night. Would it be possible for them to drive back to Philadelphia before going to Columbia, so she could get more clothes and toiletries? While taking a detour to Philadelphia was clearly not the most direct route from Detroit to Mississippi, Curtis agreed. It had been the original plan when they left for Detroit, anyway.

The next morning, Curtis and Iris headed back to Philadelphia. Even though they would be driving in the North, Curtis was still worried about being seen with a young White woman in the same car.[15] He wasn't confident that what had recently happened in Alabama couldn't happen in Ohio or western Pennsylvania as well. Just a few months earlier a White woman from Michigan, Viola Liuzzo, had been killed on a highway between Selma and Montgomery. Liuzzo had driven from her home in Detroit to Selma, where she participated in the march on Bloody Sunday. Uninjured, she stayed in Selma to participate in new marches planned for the upcoming week. After the successful march from Selma to Montgomery, Liuzzo volunteered to drive marchers in her car from Montgomery back to Selma and then return to Montgomery to fill her car with another group. While driving from Selma to Montgomery along Route 80 in Lowndes County with Leroy Moton, a nineteen-year-old Black resident of Selma who was helping her with the shuttle rides, Liuzzo realized that they were being followed. Liuzzo drove as fast as she could, but she was overtaken. As the other car passed Liuzzo's, a passenger in it fired a shot that struck her in the head, killing her instantly. As the assailants sped away, Liuzzo's car, with a horrified Moton still in the passenger seat, ran into a ditch and came to a stop. Though covered in Liuzzo's blood, Moton was uninjured and managed to turn off the engine. Now, the other car turned around and headed back toward the ditch. When the attackers approached the crashed car, Moton played dead. Looking at the motionless and bloody Luizzi and Moton, they assumed both were dead and drove away from the murder scene. After a few minutes, Moton got out of the car and flagged down another of the cars shuttling marchers back to Selma from Montgomery. Moton was driven to Selma, where he reported what had happened. He was immediately arrested by local police, but later released on bail.[16]

Media accounts of Liuzzo's murder and Moton's arrest appeared throughout the country. President Johnson asked FBI Director J. Edgar Hoover to get the FBI involved in the investigation. Hoover reported to Johnson and Attorney General Nicholas Katzenbach that Liuzzo was a drug addict with needle marks on her arm, and that at the time of the attack she and Moton had been "necking" in the car. Within twenty-four hours, four members of the KKK were arrested for murder. One of those arrested was Gary Rowe, a KKK member who had been recruited as an FBI informer. Charges against Rowe were dropped when he agreed to testify against the others. All three KKK members accused of murder were released on bail. Six weeks after the murder, a trial began for one of the accused. The jury consisted of all White males. During cross-examination of Moton, who was the key witness for the prosecution, defense counsel accused him of having "interracial sex" with Liuzzo while she was under the "hypnotic spell of narcotics." In closing argument, defense counsel described Liuzzo as "a white n—— who turned her car over to a black n—— for the purpose of hauling n——s and Communists back and forth" and Moton as a "pimp and an agent of [Fidel] Castro."[17]

After one day of deliberations, the jury returned a not guilty verdict on the murder charge but was deadlocked ten to two on the lesser charge of manslaughter, with ten jurors in favor of conviction. The surprise was not the not guilty verdict on the murder charge, but that there was almost a conviction of manslaughter. Most agreed that if Moton had been the one killed, there would have been total vindication of all charges against the accused KKK member. A retrial was held on the manslaughter charge, and once again Moton was the major prosecution witness. During cross-examination, defense counsel asked Moton whether it was "part of your duties as a transportation officer to make love to Mrs. Liuzzo." The all-White male jury in this second trial took ninety minutes to return a verdict of not guilty. In December 1965, the three accused KKK members were put on trial in federal court for the federal crime of violating Liuzzo's civil rights. All were convicted and sentenced to ten years in federal prison. After testifying at this federal trial, Moton was placed in the federal witness protection program.

All of this ran through Curtis's mind as he contemplated driving with Iris from Detroit to Philadelphia, Pennsylvania, and then down to Columbia, Mississippi. The similarities to the Liuzzo case were obvious, and Curtis was not someone to take the "it can't happen to me" attitude. Deciding that it would be best for Iris to hide on the floor in front of the back seat the car while he drove, he took a blanket from his friend's house in Detroit and placed it over Iris as she lay on the floor. Iris stayed under the blanket most of the trip back to Philadelphia. Curtis and Iris did not speak much because Curtis thought he would look suspicious talking when no one was visible in the car. When Curtis announced that he needed to stop for gasoline or a bathroom break, Iris would sit up in the back seat and take out a book she had brought with her to Washington. They thought this might make it look as if Curtis was Iris's driver. For most of the long trip, however, Iris stayed hidden under the blanket.[18] Whether this precaution had been necessary was unclear, but Curtis thought it prudent.[19]

By the end of the day, Iris and Curtis arrived at Iris's apartment in Philadelphia. Iris gathered her clothes and personal items but then realized that she had left some clothes and other items that she wanted to take with her to Mississippi at her parents' house. She decided to call home and tell her parents that she would come by the next morning to get some clothes. She had not been home since she had moved out without notice in August. As it turned out, Iris's parents knew where she had been living for some time. Eva had inquired about this from some of Iris's friends and had learned where Iris lived and what she was doing. Iris was not aware of this, nor were any family members.

That night, it occurred to Iris that she needed to tell Temple University that she was withdrawing from classes. She was unsure how long she would be in Mississippi and whether she would ever return as a student. The semester was almost finished, with final exams upcoming, and she did not want her record to show all grades of F for failing to take her finals. Iris could not find any proper stationery on which to write the withdrawal letter. The best she could come up with was the flyer from the anti–Vietnam War march in Washington that she had just attended. She turned the flyer over and wrote on the back side a letter addressed to the president of Temple University, Millard Gladfelter. In it, she first wrote that she was officially withdrawing from all her courses and requested that no grade of F be assigned to her. She then wrote that, in her opinion, attending Temple University had been a waste of her time and money. And instead of wasting more time and money, she was going to Mississippi to work with SNCC to work for the civil rights of Black people. She also condemned Temple for expanding its footprint into the surrounding neighborhood, which was uprooting many residents, most of whom were poor and Black with no place else to live. She signed the letter, placed it in an envelope addressed to the Office of the President, and dropped it in a mailbox that night. Temple never responded to her letter.

The next morning, Curtis drove Iris to her parents' home. After he parked on the street in front of the house, Iris told him to stay in the car. When Eva answered the door, Iris told her that she had quit school and was going to Mississippi to work in the civil rights movement. When Iris announced that she wished to get some of her things from her bedroom, her mother stepped out of the way as Iris walked into the house. Iris went upstairs to her former room, took some clothes and other items, and put them in a duffel bag that she had brought with her. Eva did not try to stop her or engage her in conversation. Iris's father, Morris, was not at home at the time, since he was working at the Post Office. As Iris left the house, the only thing that Eva said was "Don't bother to come back." Eva never looked out at the street as Iris walked to the car, so it is doubtful that she saw Curtis at the wheel. When Morris came back from work and learned what had happened, he was glad that Eva had told Iris not to come back. Both furious with their daughter, they now resigned themselves to the distinct possibility that they would never see her again.

With her clothes and other items from her parents' house in the car, Iris turned to Curtis and said, "I'm ready. Let's go." Curtis had been thinking more about their trip to Columbia, and he told Iris that he had changed his mind: He now had a new plan. He was very concerned about driving down to Mississippi with her; it was just too risky for a Black man to drive a young White woman through Alabama and Mississippi, even if she hid on the back-seat floor again. If anyone saw her in the car, Curtis could be stopped and arrested for kidnapping, rape, pimping, or some other made-up charge. No matter what Iris told the police, Curtis would be in serious trouble, perhaps lynched. He also worried that Iris's parents would report to the police that she had been kidnapped.

Curtis outlined to Iris his new plan. He remembered Iris telling him about the family in Savannah with whom she had lived the past summer with SCOPE. Now they would drive straight from Philadelphia to Savannah, without the need to sleep over anywhere. Curtis had friends with whom he could stay in Savannah for a night. He then would drive from Savannah to Columbia by himself; Iris would stay in Savannah for a few days, until he was back in Columbia, then travel to Columbia by herself. This would be much safer.

On the one hand, Iris was happy that she would be seeing her host family from the summer. She knew that they would be happy to see her as well. On the other hand, she was worried that Curtis was dumping her in Savannah, and that she would never hear from him again, and never have another chance to join SNCC in Columbia. She didn't truly think that was the case, but after all, she had just met him a few days before, and things had moved quite quickly, to say the least. But, seeing no other options, Iris agreed that the new plan made good sense. The risks of being seen with Curtis in a car somewhere in the Deep South were simply too great to ignore.

Fortunately, the drive from Philadelphia to Savannah went without incident. Curtis did most of the driving, but Iris drove for a couple short stints as well. When Iris was driving, Curtis hid on the back-seat floor, and only when Iris was at the wheel did they stop for gas. Bathroom breaks were arranged so that Curtis would not encounter segregated facilities. Iris tried to contact her host family in Savannah before arriving, but her call would not go through. She considered the possibility that they had moved, but she figured that she knew several neighbors well enough that she could likely stay with them if necessary. In any event, her concerns were unfounded: When she and Curtis arrived at the house, the host family greeted her happily and had no problem with her staying with them a few nights. Curtis told Iris he would call her in a few days to arrange when she should take a bus to Hattiesburg, the closest city to Columbia with regular bus service. When he left, Iris still wasn't sure if she'd ever see him again.

Curtis stayed that night just outside Savannah with a friend from SNCC, and the next day drove to Columbia by himself. Two days later, he called Iris and told her to take the bus to Hattiesburg the following day. The next day Iris boarded the bus to her first stop, Atlanta, as directed. Once in Hattiesburg, she called Curtis from a pay phone at the bus station. Curtis soon arrived, and he and Iris were relieved to see one another. The time had come for Iris's civil rights story to move on to Columbia, Mississippi.

CHAPTER 9

Columbia, Mississippi

COLUMBIA LIES ALONG THE PEARL River in Marion County, Mississippi, about thirty-five miles west of Hattiesburg, eighty miles south of the capital city of Jackson, and one hundred miles north of New Orleans. It was founded by settlers who had moved there from Columbia, South Carolina—hence the town's name—several years before Mississippi became a state in 1817. Some who relocated brought their enslaved human property with them. Columbia had served as the county seat for many years; the county courthouse, its most distinctive building, stands at the center of downtown.

In the mid-1960s Columbia had a population of approximately seven thousand, divided somewhat equally between Black and White. The town was racially segregated in all aspects of life,[1] with Black and White people living in separated neighborhoods. The White neighborhoods had paved streets and paved sidewalks. The Black ones had dirt roads without sidewalks. Downtown, a burger stand sold hamburgers to both Black and White customers, but only Whites were served at the front window; Black customers had to go to the side of the store and order at the window marked "Colored." There was a movie theater across from the courthouse that admitted both Black and White people, but Black patrons could only sit in the balcony and were only permitted to enter the theater through a back door, adjacent to a stairwell leading to the balcony. They were not allowed in the theater's lobby to purchase popcorn or other snacks, or to use the bathrooms in the theater. There was also a dentist's office downtown. While the White dentist did treat Black patients, they had to enter through a back door and sit in the "colored waiting room," which had rickety wood floors and hard wooden benches. Black people could not make a prior appointment at the dental office; instead, they had to wait until the dentist had an opening. Any White patient walking in would be treated first, no matter how long a Black patient had already waited. Sometimes a Black patient waited the whole day without being treated and had to return the next day. At downtown clothing stores, Black customers could not try on any clothes or return any items purchased, no matter the reason.[2] Columbia had a public swimming pool, but when town officials learned that that they could no longer legally exclude Black people from using it, they had the pool drained and shut it down. The public schools were also segregated, and Black schools were severely underfunded. Many White residents of the town (how many is unclear) belonged to the KKK, and Columbia's KKK chapter included prominent businessmen. Very few Black people in town were registered to vote. When those who were registered tried to vote, White officials treated them as if they were attempting to break the law, which naturally dissuaded many registered Black voters from going to the polls.

The mayor of Columbia at the time was Earl "Buddy" McLean.[3] He entered the mayor's office in 1965 at the age of forty. He had lived in Columbia since early childhood, his parents having moved with him from North Carolina. He went back to North Carolina to attend Duke University, but after graduation he returned to Columbia where he entered the insurance business, married, and was an active member of the Columbia Presbyterian Church. During his mayoral campaign McLean sought the support of both White and Black voters. He walked both Black and White neighborhoods, knocking on doors to introduce himself to residents as a candidate for mayor. McLean thought it was important that Columbia avoid the violence and racial tensions experienced by other small towns in Mississippi. He warned his would-be constituents about Columbia becoming another Philadelphia, Mississippi, or McComb. Once in office, he agreed to the formation of a biracial committee that had been sought by many civil rights activists. But the biracial committee McLean formed came under criticism for only choosing Black members others considered "Uncle Toms" because they had never taken part in the civil rights movement or shown any interest in the issues most important to the Black community. Unlike the mayors in many other Mississippi towns,

McLean was at least not hostile to the Black community; however, one could not say that he succeeded in convincing many others in Columbia to adopt a similar attitude. As I was told years later,[4] there was "no room" for any White liberals in Columbia: "You were either on one side or the other." The "decent" White community did "precious little" to challenge Jim Crow, notwithstanding Mayor McLean's hope for the town.

Curtis was the first SNCC worker to come to Columbia. In spring 1965 he had been working for SNCC in Biloxi and then Hattiesburg when the SNCC headquarters in Atlanta contacted him. SNCC's research staff had concluded that the Columbia area was a promising area to target for economic growth and political organization. Its demographic comprised a 40 percent voting-age Black population, which presented an opportunity for political change. SNCC staff recommended allocating significant resources to Columbia, based on its belief that if they could defeat racism in Mississippi, other states would follow. They therefore asked Curtis to move to Columbia and begin the community organization process, the key to SNCC's approach. Curtis agreed to do so.

Since SNCC had no infrastructure in place in Columbia when Curtis arrived there, he had to begin the process from scratch. SNCC provided him with the names of several people it had identified as possible supporters but warned him that there was no guarantee that any of those on the list would be willing to help. SNCC leaders harbored some concern that Curtis might encounter hostility toward SNCC, even among the Black community. Additionally, there was the likelihood of police harassment and KKK violence against both Curtis and those on his list. Therefore, they developed a plan. Curtis would carry the names and addresses of prospective SNCC supporters "in code." Only he and SNCC headquarters knew the code. In this way, if the police arrested Curtis, no one on the list would be implicated in SNCC's plans.

When Curtis first traveled to Columbia, he arrived by bus after dark. He did not think it wise to try to contact anyone that night, so he spent the night in the woods. The next morning, he walked to the home of the first name on his encoded list, the Dukes family, who lived on Hendrick Street in a small house, one of the nicer ones in the Black section of town. They also owned another house, better described as a shack, a couple blocks away at 623 Nathan Street. The Nathan Street house had no indoor toilet—only an outhouse—and no indoor shower or bath, though it did have a kitchen sink, stove, and refrigerator. The house was heated by a wood stove. Curtis agreed to rent the Nathan Street shack, which became known as SNCC's Columbia Freedom House and the center of civil rights activity in Columbia and surrounding Marion County.

For the first couple days, Curtis lived alone at the house. He chopped wood out back for firewood and quietly walked around the Black neighborhood, introducing himself to those he came across. He tracked down the others on his coded list, all of whom seemed supportive of SNCC's efforts in Columbia. Others offered Curtis a place to stay, but he decided to remain at the Nathan Street house. Three days after Curtis arrived in Columbia, a large, strong Black man knocked on the door as he was eating breakfast. The man, Willis Johnson McClenton, known as W.J., was forty years old and earned his living as a truck driver, hauling pulpwood. He'd quit school after the third grade. When Curtis opened the door, W.J. announced, "My name is W.J. McClenton. I just quit my job. I am here to fight for freedom." W.J. had seen Curtis walking around the neighborhood and was told that he was working for civil rights and freedom for Black people. Curtis told W.J. that he had come to the right place and invited him inside. After a brief conversation, W.J. accepted Curtis's invitation to move into the Nathan Street Freedom House.[5] Thus began the SNCC team in Columbia.

At this time, the Democratic Party in Mississippi shunned Black members, and thus barred Black people from voting in primary elections. With support from several civil rights organizations, including SNCC, the Mississippi Freedom Democratic Party (MFDP) was formed. This, of course, was the organization whose delegates had sought to be seated at the 1964 DNC convention, the site of Iris's first experience with the civil rights movement. Curtis and W.J. worked to build the MFDP in Marion County from their Nathan Street house. During the summer of 1964, groups of White students from several northern colleges came to Columbia to help Curtis and W.J. with their efforts on behalf of the MFDP. These students frequently stayed at the Nathan Street house, sleeping on the floor in sleeping bags they had been advised to bring with them. The college students not only helped with voter registration but also taught in the Freedom Schools that SNCC established in town for both children and adults. The Freedom Schools taught not only literacy but also Black history.[6] The student volunteers, along with Curtis and W.J., also helped establish a library for Black people with books donated from northern libraries and individual supporters.

Curtis and W.J. not only oversaw the college volunteers but busily worked on their own projects. They followed the SNCC pattern of spending time in the local Black community, meeting with local leaders of churches and businesses, and talking with regular people on the streets. They also went door-to-door to seek support for the mass meetings SNCC held. SNCC always played the long game to gain the trust of the community and to achieve SNCC's ultimate goal of developing local leadership.

At the end of July 1964, however, one of SNCC's great fears was realized. At 1:00 a.m. Sunday morning someone firebombed the Nathan Street house and gunshots rang out, leaving fourteen bullet holes in the front screen. Seven bullets made it to the back wall of the building. Investigators later found plastic bleach bottles filled with gasoline on the front porch. Although the building sustained heavy damage, no one was injured.[7] News of the bombing and shooting made national news. The UPI wire service story identified the building as one housing several civil rights workers, including "one Negro," Curtis Styles of Biloxi, and four White college students. The story also mentioned that the FBI had joined the local police in the investigation into the incident.[8] An article in the local *Hattiesburg American* newspaper mentioned that Curtis had been in Columbia for about a month, while the others had arrived later. All had a connection with the MFDP. The house, it was reported, was a "frame residence" owned by Roberta Dukes in the "Negro quarter."[9] A slightly different spin was provided by *The Columbian-Progress*, Columbia's local newspaper: "A fire of more than passing interest was brought under control by Columbia's efficient fire department. There was some damage, but generally speaking the firemen were credited with saving the house." The article continued that the house was "occupied by a group of out-of-towners," and that the cause of the fire "is not known." The article listed the residents as two White women, two White men, and one Negro. All five were named along with their hometowns or colleges.[10] Shortly after the attack on the Freedom House, the four White students returned to their colleges. W.J. and Curtis bravely remained in the house, cleaning it up and replacing the windows. No one was ever identified as responsible for the firebombing or shooting, and no arrests were ever made.

SNCC continued to support W.J. and Curtis throughout the summer and fall of 1964. That December Curtis, as director of the Columbia project, determined that he needed more help, especially from someone with experience that would not require close supervision. In January 1965 he went to a MFDP conference in Hattiesburg. There he met Ira Grupper. After speaking with Ira, Curtis knew that this was the person he wanted to bring to Columbia. He spent the next few days trying to convince Ira to move to Columbia.

Ira Grupper was born in Brooklyn and raised in an Orthodox Jewish home, although after his bar mitzvah at age thirteen he no longer followed his religious upbringing. He and his family lived in a public housing project. After graduating high school, Ira attended Brooklyn College, but he dropped out during his freshman year and moved to Atlanta to work for SNCC, where he was assigned to the research department. His interest in the civil rights movement stemmed from the student lunch counter sit-ins at a Woolworth's store in Greensboro, North Carolina, which happened while he was still a high school student in Brooklyn. After reading about these sit-ins in the newspaper, Ira's father took him to Woolworth's in their neighborhood to demonstrate their support for the Greensboro students. There Ira and his father joined with others, almost all working-class Jews, and walked a picket line outside the store. Ira was moved by the fact that during their protest almost no one crossed the picket line to enter the store. It was at this moment that he saw the power that mass movement direct action could have to improve the world.[11]

Ira enjoyed his research work for SNCC in Atlanta, looking for new locations where SNCC might improve conditions for Black residents. Columbia was not one of the locations that he had evaluated. After he had spent a couple years of working for the research department at the main office, SNCC officials, impressed with the work product, sincerity, enthusiasm, and spirit of this skinny young Jewish man from Brooklyn, asked him if he would be willing to go to Hattiesburg, Mississippi, to work with the Council of Federated Organizations (COFO), the coalition formed in 1962 when SNCC project director

Bob Moses convinced officials from the NAACP, CORE, and SCLC to join SNCC to work together in a new umbrella organization. Ira agreed to work with COFO in Hattiesburg on voter registration, political education, and economic fairness issues. While there, Ira also worked with the MFDP in its registration efforts and toward its goal of creating an alternative political party in Mississippi. After meeting Ira at the Hattiesburg conference in January 1965, Curtis contacted SNCC headquarters and named Ira as the person he wanted to bring to Columbia. SNCC headquarters approved Ira's transfer, and within a few months he joined Curtis and W.J. at the Nathan Street Freedom House, where all three lived together, sleeping on mattresses on the floor.

The three men worked indefatigably together throughout the summer and fall. Because Ira was White, he could more easily navigate the White area of town and talk with White people who seemed sympathetic, or at least not openly hostile, to SNCC's presence. One such person worked in a downtown retail store. This person provided information to Ira about which White store owners were especially hostile to Black customers. He also provided names of people he suspected of possible KKK membership—a list that included businessmen, public officials, police officers, and church officials—and told Ira which times were busiest at each store, when deliveries were expected, and the times when the owners were there. Ira used this information to decide which stores to picket, on what days, and at what times. Another person who helped Ira was a fourteen-year-old White student who one day showed up at the Nathan Street house and told Ira and Curtis that he wanted to help. At first they were concerned that the boy was some type of spy sent to gain information about upcoming SNCC activities. They also worried that they were being set up for accusations of providing drugs or alcohol to or engaging in sexual activity with this teenager. But they were wrong. He worked hard to support them by passing out circulars about SNCC programs, knocking on doors and encouraging people to attend neighborhood meetings, and personally participating in marches. After several weeks, however, the young volunteer stopped coming by the Freedom House. Nor was he seen around town. When Ira asked about him, he was told that his parents, displeased with their son's association with Ira, had sent him to live with family members in Hattiesburg. Ira never heard from him again.

Meanwhile Ira, Curtis, and W.J. led several attempts to integrate segregated businesses, usually without incident but also without much success. One such attempt was at Autry's Café in the downtown business district. Autry's was a local hangout for White workers, some of whom belonged to the KKK. The trio persuaded four Black men to enter the café and try to order food. As expected, the four were denied service and pretty much ignored. After about an hour of waiting to be served, the Black men left peacefully. Most likely, the café owner had been given advance warning of the integration attempt and had instructed everyone inside not to create any problems.

The week after Thanksgiving 1965, Curtis returned to Columbia with the donated car he had picked up in Detroit. Curtis told Ira and W.J. that he had met a nineteen-year-old woman who attended Temple University at an antiwar rally in Washington. He described her as White, Jewish, very sincere, and willing to work hard. She had worked with SCLC's SCOPE project the past summer in Savannah but was disappointed in how little she had accomplished. She had worked with several SNCC workers in Americus, Georgia, and now she wanted to work with SNCC in Mississippi. She would be arriving shortly from Savannah, where Curtis had driven her from Detroit, to join their group.

Neither Ira nor W.J. thought this was a good idea. The house was already crowded enough, with the three of them, without a nineteen-year-old female moving in. Women had stayed over at the house before, but they had been part of several groups on short-term visits. Never had one female stayed alone with them. They asked Curtis if his interest in Iris was more personal than SNCC-related, but he was adamant that it was not; he thought it would be a good idea to add a woman to the team. Ira and W.J. only reluctantly agreed.

When Iris arrived at the Nathan Street Freedom House, she asked herself, "What have I gotten myself into?" The house in which she was to live had recently been bombed. Its walls were charred. There were bullet holes in the walls. The front porch had collapsed; you had to climb over cinder blocks to get to the front door. The "bathroom" was an outhouse, and the bedding consisted of four well-worn mattresses on the floor—which one was hers was not yet clear. On the plus side, the broken windows that were shot out had been replaced, and there was an indoor kitchen sink and a working kitchen. There was also a working telephone on the wall. Iris consoled herself by saying "I am now part of SNCC."

Curtis, Ira, and W.J. told Iris they had big plans for the next day. Was she was willing to join them and local residents in picketing Lampton's, a downtown department store that refused to hire Black people? Now this was exactly what she had come for! "Absolutely," she replied. There was a possibility that she would be arrested, so they gave her the telephone number of an attorney who would help if legal assistance became necessary.

The next day, Iris's first full one in Columbia, she went along with her three new roommates to Lampton's Department Store, which stood on the corner of the two main downtown streets, across from the courthouse. Outside Lampton's, they met up with a group of local Black residents. Carrying signs with different wording, but the same message—"Hire Black Workers"—they chanted and sang songs now quite familiar to Iris on the sidewalk in front of the store. After a while the manager of Lampton's came out and asked them to stop demonstrating, a request the demonstrators ignored. Shortly thereafter, the Columbia police arrived. When one of the officers asked to speak with the leaders of the demonstration, Curtis, Ira, and W.J. stepped forward. After a short hesitation, Iris, too, joined them. The police officer said that if they did not disperse immediately, everyone would be arrested for trespassing. Curtis told the officer that they had the right to demonstrate peacefully. At that, the officer proceeded to arrest the three men, but not Iris. As Curtis, Ira, and W.J. were handcuffed and placed in the paddy wagon, Iris realized that she was now alone in a town where she had just arrived the day before, and that she would be sleeping that night—and who knew how many more—by herself in a bombed-out shack in a Black neighborhood in a small rural town in Mississippi. While getting into the paddy wagon, Curtis called out, telling her to call the lawyer whose number they had given her.

Walking as quickly as she could back to Nathan Street, Iris was scared but tried her best not to cry. She called the lawyer and told him what had happened. He said that the three men would be held in jail until bail was posted, but he could not help her get bail money. Nor did he know anyone who could. He suggested that she call around to raise money from others. When she told him that she knew no one to contact because she had just arrived in Columbia, he said he was sorry, but he could not be of any help. Despondent, Iris walked back to the jail to report the bad news. She was not allowed inside the jail, however, so she could not speak with her housemates now in custody.

Upon arrest, Ira had been placed in a "White" cell by himself, while Curtis and W.J. were placed together in a "Negro" cell. The two cells were adjacent, but their respective occupants could not see each other. Other than being labeled as racially segregated cells, they were identical, particularly in their filthy condition. Soon after being locked up, Curtis, W.J., and Ira began to sing the popular civil rights song "Ain't Gonna Let Nobody Turn Me 'Round." They were soon joined in song by supporters outside the courthouse jail who had followed them after their arrest and could hear their singing. Back from her unsuccessful attempt to procure legal help, Iris joined the crowd. After a short time, the sheriff ordered the prisoners to quit singing "or else." It was not clear what "or else" meant, but they did not want to find out. The prisoners stopped singing, but not those out on the street. As day turned to night, the demonstrators outside the courthouse began to trickle home. Curtis, W.J., and Ira realized that they were not going to get bailed out and would be staying the night.

As the crowd dispersed outside the county courthouse, Iris returned to the Nathan Street house. She had been in Columbia for roughly twenty-four hours, and now she found herself all alone. With no idea what to do, she sat by herself in the house, almost in shock with fear. Then there was a knock on the door. When she opened it, a young Black woman, eighteen years of age, introduced herself as Margie. Margie had been at the Lampton's demonstration earlier in the day, and among the crowd at the courthouse after the arrests. She saw that Iris was with Curtis, W.J., and Ira, so she had followed her back to Nathan Street after everyone else went home. Margie told Iris that she had recently moved out of her parents' house on a nearby street and now lived in a house by herself. She invited Iris to stay with her, and Iris gratefully accepted the offer. At least she would not have to spend the night alone, and Margie seemed nice and sincere in her offer to help. Iris packed some personal items and a change of clothes and walked back with Margie to her one-room cinder-block house. The house had no running water. There was an outhouse out back, and inside there was one electrical outlet into which a small lamp, with a single lightbulb, but no shade, was plugged. Margie told Iris that she should not stay at the Nathan Street Freedom House by herself, and that she was welcome to stay with Margie as long as she wanted. Iris agreed to stay until Curtis, Ira, and W.J. got out of jail.

Margie introduced Iris to many people who lived in the area, including the Daniels family. After Iris had been with Margie for about a week, the family invited Iris to move in with them. Their home was also made of cinder blocks, but it had a sink with running water. It, too, had no indoor toilet, only an outhouse. Although the house was larger than Margie's, the Daniels had twelve children living with them, so it was not as if Iris was moving to more spacious quarters, but she did not want to take advantage of Margie's generosity by staying too long. For the next week, Iris didn't do much but hang around the house and help with the younger children.

Two weeks after their arrest, Curtis, Ira, and W.J. were released from jail. At this point, Iris moved out of the Daniels' house and returned to the Nathan Street Freedom House. All three men, especially Curtis, apologized to her for leaving her to fend for herself the day after her arrival in Columbia. Iris tried to downplay the stress she had experienced, saying she was certain her situation did not compare to that which the three of them had experienced in jail. The experience ended up bringing Iris closer to Curtis, Ira, and W.J. She had gained their trust and respect by staying in Columbia during their jail time, proving that she was truly committed to the civil rights movement and not just some flaky nineteen-year-old running away from home.

Now Ira made a special effort to get to know Iris. During their conversations, she told him about her broken relationship with her parents. Ira suggested that he reach out to her mother, Eva, and try to patch things up, and Iris agreed. In the letter Ira sent to her mother, he introduced himself as a Jewish boy from New York who had worked in the civil rights movement on a full-time basis for several years. He told Eva that he would look after Iris while she worked with him and the others. He wrote that there were many very nice people in Columbia, that he would make sure Iris was safe, and that he, like Iris, was committed to equal rights for everyone. Black people in the South had been treated unfairly for many years, he told Eva. Lots of White students, many of them Jewish, were working to effect this change. He added that he felt that as Jews they had a special reason to fight for people facing discrimination at the hands of the state and fellow citizens. Ira added their address in Columbia, hoping that Eva would write back to him. He closed his letter saying that he looked forward to meeting her someday.

Ira's letter was clearly an attempt to temper Eva's opposition to Iris's presence in Mississippi. It made no mention of the two Black men with whom Iris also lived, and could even be read as implying that Ira, a Jewish boy from New York, was romantically interested in Iris. Perhaps this might make it easier for Eva to accept her daughter's decision.

About two weeks after Ira mailed the letter, Eva's response arrived in the mail. In it, she thanked Ira for his concern for Iris, but said she still worried about Iris's safety, considering what had happened to Andrew Goodman and Michael Schwerner, the two Jewish boys from New York killed the year before in Philadelphia, Mississippi. Eva included a $10 bill in the envelope. As it turned out, thus began a regular line of communication between Iris and her mother. Eva sent $10 every week, and every week Iris called Eva from a pay phone on the street. She never mentioned Curtis or W.J.; the weekly calls served solely to assure her mother that she was well. Eva sent canisters of powdered milk to share with Ira. The fact that Eva stayed in regular contact with Iris when she was in Columbia, Mississippi, was something she never told any of our family members. I only learned of this when I interviewed Iris and Ira over fifty years later.

Curtis, Ira, and W.J. were protective of Iris and typically gave her the "safer" assignments. Iris contacted the group Conscience at Temple University to ask for help in raising funds for the SNCC project in Columbia, which led to some financial support. Her past relationship with Conscience also led to her recruitment of three of the group's members, all Black women, who ended up working in Columbia for a couple weeks before the start of the spring semester. Besides fundraising and recruitment, Iris worked on community projects. She especially enjoyed working on issues involving education. For example, she met with a member of the local Board of Education, a White man, to discuss the disparity of funding between the public schools for Whites and those for Black people; White public schools in Columbia received five times more money per student than their Black counterparts. Iris also spoke with Black parents to encourage them to enroll their children in White schools. When one family agreed to send their daughter to a White school, Iris regularly visited the family to see how they were doing, and sympathized with them when they told her of the racial slurs that their daughter encountered. Knowing that a White woman cared about their child provided some degree of solace to the family in their courageous stand against segregated schools.

In addition to trying to improve the situation in the public schools, Iris worked with the local chapter of the MFDP to identify local Black residents who might be interested in serving in political leadership roles, canvass Black neighborhoods in support of MFDP's policies, and encourage political participation. She tried to convince people to run for political office by discussing political organization and campaigning. She also worked to help local residents start their own businesses, especially women. For example, when visiting a woman in her home, Iris might admire the beautiful quilts that the woman had made, then encourage her to open her own business selling quilts and other hand-sewn items such as decorative pillows and throw rugs. She held classes on financial literacy, teaching others about checking accounts, invoices, and simple accounting. She arranged meetings for women business owners with the local office of the federal Small Business Administration, so they could learn about the ins and outs of obtaining federal financial assistance for their new businesses. She also helped them explore local and state government opportunities for getting small business loans. For those Black women not interested in opening and operating their own business, Iris helped them seek paid employment. She encouraged women to apply for jobs that they previously would not have considered—for example, as salespeople at White-owned retail stores—and met with the White owners of businesses in town to talk to them about opening their hiring process to Black women. Iris was a constant presence in the homes of Black women, offering them encouragement and support and urging them to embrace new economic and political opportunities.

In addition to all these activities, Iris worked on local agricultural issues. SNCC helped organize agricultural cooperatives to help small farmers sell their crops. Following the lead of Cesar Chavez in California, SNCC worked to organize farm workers in Marion County into a union. SNCC held meetings with Black farm workers during which they screened film strips produced in California showing the violence suffered by Mexican farm workers. The message was clear:

Farm workers in Mississippi needed a labor union every bit as much as the farm workers in California did. Iris was also involved with SNCC efforts before the US Department of Agriculture's Agricultural Stabilization and Conservation Committees to eliminate racial discrimination in decisions regarding the number of acres that individual farmers were allowed to plant.[12] Demands were also presented to government agencies to stop discrimination in distribution of food stamps, welfare benefits, and crop subsidies.

SNCC constantly pressed local government officials to create a biracial committee that would promote cooperation between White and Black residents on matters of mutual economic interest. Despite the efforts of Curtis, W.J., Ira, and Iris, and the support of some local officials, including Mayor McLean, disagreements over the composition of such a committee and the general mistrust between the White and Black communities were too great to overcome, and Columbia never created a biracial committee during this time.

Iris found her work with SNCC in Columbia very gratifying; she was always busy working on a project that she felt was important. This is not to say that her efforts were always successful. Indeed, many of her and SNCC's goals for the issues they tried to improve fell short. It should also be noted that as hard as Iris worked, Curtis, Ira, and W.J. worked just as hard, if not harder. Busy every day from morning until evening, they were a continuous presence in the Black community, consistent with SNCC's approach to community organizing. Additionally, all four attended church services every Sunday. This showed their sincerity and support for the local community. Afterward, they typically spoke with other church attendees and usually took one of them up on an invitation to their home for a meal or just to talk. For that matter, all four of them ate a good many home-cooked meals with residents and their families during any given week.

Clearly, the community embraced and supported Iris and her fellow SNCC workers. Nevertheless, as civil rights workers in Mississippi, they never truly felt safe. It had, after all, only been a few months since the Nathan Street Freedom House firebombing. For this reason, they placed the mattresses on which they slept directly under the windowsills to lessen the chance of being hit by a bullet coming through the window while they slept. None of the four ventured outside the Black area at night. Moreover, those whom they supported were also concerned about their own safety. Some in the community admitted that they were hesitant to invite Iris, Curtis, Ira, or W.J. into their homes for fear that they might be targeted. Others worried about losing their job for openly supporting SNCC workers. Fortunately, during Iris's time in Columbia, even though White night riders sought to intimidate Black people in their neighborhood, no violent attacks took place.

From the time of Curtis's arrival in Columbia, the SNCC workers were under constant surveillance. At first it was local police cars that drove slowly by the house several times a day and at night. Then they noticed private vehicles slowing down outside the Freedom House. It then became apparent that their mail was being opened. Although nothing was taken from the envelopes, including Eva's $10 bills, it was obvious that someone had opened the envelope and removed and inspected the contents. It later came out that the FBI had run a surveillance program targeting civil rights groups.[13] It is doubtful that the FBI obtained any useful information on the group in Columbia, but it was disconcerting nevertheless to be the targets of such surveillance.

At some point, the four mattresses once arranged against each of the house's four walls lay under only three windows. Iris and Curtis had begun sleeping next to one another. As Ira described it to me years later, they had "become an item." The timeline of this budding romance is not clear. As Iris put it to me, "It just happened." Their relationship certainly was a strictly platonic one when Iris first arrived in Columbia, but during their time together there, the nature of their relationship changed.[14] That said, their romantic relationship was only manifest inside the four walls of Freedom House. They took great care never to let on that they were romatically involved in public: they never held hands, looked into each other's eyes for more than a moment, or interacted in playful ways in public. Only Ira and W.J. knew of their relationship. One telling sign of Iris's romantic relationship with Curtis was what happened—or didn't happen—when several female students from a northern university came to Columbia to show their support for SNCC activities, and stayed in the Nathan Street Freedom House for a few nights. This was not an unusual occurrence. What was unusual was Curtis's lack of interest in, shall we say, getting to know these women. This had never been the case for Curtis or Ira with past female visitors.

CHAPTER 10

Greenville Air Force Base

IN MID-JANUARY 1966, MISSISSIPPI WAS very cold. Iris reflected on how hot and steamy Savannah had been during her initial trip to the South. She had formed the misconception that it was always warm in the South, but now, as the temperatures in Columbia dropped into the teens at night and barely got above freezing during the day, she came to know better. Living without air conditioning had been bad enough in the summer in Savannah; living with no central heat in Mississippi during a winter freezing spell was worse—and more dangerous. Iris, Ira, W.J., and Curtis tried to warm the Freedom House on Nathan Street by burning wood in the stove. All four wore several layers of clothes, sweaters, and jackets day and night inside the house. They were cold and uncomfortable, but they were better off than many Black residents in the rural Mississippi Delta, many of whom lived on former plantations in unheated shacks with broken windows. Opportunities for decent housing for Black people in the Delta were just about nonexistent. They lived in extreme poverty, with a median annual income of $456. Ninety percent of their houses had no indoor toilets or baths. Over half of the Black men over the age of twenty-five in the Delta had less than a sixth-grade education, which limited job opportunities.[1]

Many Black residents of the Delta were unemployed, their former jobs picking cotton made obsolete by new technology. And once those jobs were gone, no new job opportunities opened. Moreover, among other things, extreme poverty led to inadequate diets, which exacerbated their problems. Although federal poverty programs existed, meant to ameliorate the problems created by abject poverty, local officials refused to cooperate in providing the available benefits to poor Black people. For example, a program run by the federal Office of Economic Opportunity (OEO), Operation Help, had offered to hire five hundred unemployed people to distribute surplus food to the poor.[2] But because of the program's requirement to hire a certain number of Black residents, most local governments in Mississippi refused to participate in Operation Help. The local governments tried to defend their position by arguing that participation in the federal program would violate local laws requiring that all public employees be White.

In response to these sorts of barriers, a new group was organized. A coalition of members of the Mississippi Freedom Democratic Party, the Mississippi Freedom Labor Union, and the Delta Ministry, the civil rights arm of the National Council of Churches, it called itself the Poor People's Conference. Unaffiliated individual activists also joined. The Poor People's Conference was convened at the end of January in Edwards, Mississippi, near Jackson.[3] There its members discussed the plight of the local Black residents and the refusal of local governments to provide them with help. Those present shared emotional stories of people living in rickety shacks with snow falling through holes in the roofs, and of families without adequate food to feed their children. Many were appalled to learn that two Black residents had frozen to death the previous week not far from where they were meeting. All assembled agreed that appeals to government officials, even federal officials, were a waste of time. Moreover, the weather was too cold to hold a march in protest. What to do? After much discussion, they agreed that the most important immediate goal was to get all of the local residents a safe, warm place to live. They developed a plan: Occupy the abandoned Greenville Air Force Base in Greenville, Mississippi, about one hundred miles away, where they might be able to house everyone that needed safe shelter.[4]

Acting pursuant to the Poor People's Conference plan, on Monday, January 31, 1966, at about 6:30 a.m., forty people, most of them Black, entered the Greenville Air Force Base, which had been shuttered due to budget cuts, by cutting through a perimeter fence. The group's entrance onto the base at first went unnoticed by the small contingent of civilian guards protecting it; no one had ever tried to enter the base since its closing three years earlier. The group entered an unlocked former barracks building, where they posted a sign that they had brought with them: "This is our home—please knock before entering."[5] The private security guards soon alerted Air Force Command to the presence of the intruders. Upon notification, Air Force Lieutenant Colonel George Andrews got to the base quickly. He went to the barracks and spoke to the group, ordering everyone to leave. "You are trespassing on Government property," he said, in violation of federal law.

Anticipating such a confrontation, the occupiers had prepared a statement and written demands that they read aloud to Andrews. The statement began with the heading "Why We Are Here at Greenville Air Force Base."[6] It went on to explain:

> We are here because we are hungry and cold and have no jobs or land. We don't want charity. We are willing to work for ourselves if given a chance.
>
> We are at the Greenville Air Force Base because it is federal property and there are hundreds of empty houses and buildings. We need those houses and the land. We could be trained for jobs in the buildings.

The group's demands then became more specific: First, they needed food, especially for their children, who could not learn in school because of constant hunger. Their local schools had no free breakfast or free lunch programs, unlike White schools. The Black schools did sell food, but the children's parents lacked the money to buy it. Second, the group demanded jobs. Many of the occupiers had been evicted from the plantations on which they had worked all their lives. "We don't want charity," they emphasized. "We demand our rights to jobs, so that we can do something with our lives and build us a future." This led to the third demand—job training. Poor people, they posited, should receive paid job training to learn new skills and gain employment. Fourth, they demanded direct relief payments for the purchase of decent and adequate amounts of food to keep themselves and their families alive. The government surplus food they had received was "unfit" to eat, "old . . . full of bugs . . . and weevils."[7] They wanted fresh vegetables, fruit, and meat. They wanted the power to decide for themselves which foods to eat, not be forced to eat whatever the government was trying to unload. In the past, whenever they complained to the federal agencies, they were told to go to local agencies for help. But when local officials were asked for help, they denied knowledge of any available government aid programs. The protesters wanted Operation Help to stop relying on Mississippi county boards—which simply refused to do their job under the program—to distribute food; these boards did not represent the interests of the poor Black people of Mississippi, and therefore they should not decide who to serve or what food to offer. Finally, the protesters demanded land. The core reason for their poverty—and for the fact that they were now occupying the barracks—was that they owned no land. Thousands of acres of federal land were going unused by the government. The protesters offered to clear, farm, and otherwise develop some of this land themselves, and make it productive. This would also create jobs and income for the area's poor people.

After hearing this impassioned plea, Lieutenant Colonel Andrews had a simple response: "My only concern is with this building."[8] There was nothing that he could say or could do about their demands, he told the group, and ordered them to leave the barracks. When no one budged, Andrews left the building, ignoring a kick to his shin from one member of the group as he made his way out.

While Andrews was inside the barracks, listening to the group's demands, a contingent of local law enforcement officers had arrived at the base. They were instructed not to enter the occupied barracks. After his meeting with the occupiers, he went to the local police chief, W. C. Burnley, and told him what he had just learned. Responding that he had no jurisdiction over this dispute because it was on federal property, Burnley immediately ordered his men to disperse. Obeying their chief's order, they left the base, allowing the occupiers to remain inside the barracks. Now Andrews returned to his office and reported the situation to his superiors in Washington, including Air Force chief of staff General John P. McConnell. Word of the base occupation then reached the White House.

Around 11:00 a.m., about fifteen more protesters arrived at the barracks, bringing coal stoves, food, mattresses, and blankets. Throughout the day, more people arrived with more supplies. By early afternoon Air Force Police officers had arrived at the base and tried to stop all traffic at the front gate, but they were not successful; many people managed to gain access to the base and the barracks through side and back entrances. An official from the federal Civil Rights Commission, alerted by Air Force officials, then contacted the Delta Ministry to ask what was happening at the base. Upon being told that two people in the area had frozen to death the prior week, and that others had no food or place to stay safely out of the extreme cold, the Civil Rights Commission official responded that these problems did not justify breaking the law.

Recognizing that no help would be forthcoming from either federal or local government officials, the occupiers concluded that their control of the barracks would need to be long-term. About 2:00 p.m., an election was held to select leaders to organize the group and negotiate with government and military officials. The elected leaders divided everyone into several committees, charged variously with cleaning the barracks, preparing meals, and arranging sleeping plans. Later that afternoon, more people arrived at the barracks. Around 7:30 p.m., everyone enjoyed a spaghetti dinner prepared by the meal committee. Throughout the evening, more people bearing supplies continued to arrive. During the night, groups took turns sleeping on mattresses spread out on the floor and staying awake to keep watch.

Back in Columbia, late in the afternoon of January 31, Curtis received word from the MFDP office in Hattiesburg of the events in Greenville. He decided to join the group the next day, and Iris agreed to join him. Their plan was to leave Columbia about 6:00 a.m. the next day to make the approximately two-hundred-mile drive to the base. They collected clothes, blankets, and food from some neighbors and packed them into their car for the trip the next morning. Luckily, the weather, although very cold, was clear, and they made the drive to Greenville without incident. When they arrived, they managed to enter the base through an opening in the perimeter fence that someone had created the day before. Prior to entering the base, Iris and Curtis saw a contingent of journalists eager to interview the protesters, but the military police had denied the press entry onto the base. The journalists stood outside the fence, hoping for news of what was happening inside the barracks.

Once inside the occupied barracks, Curtis recognized a few friends from MFDC. He and Iris went over to them and expressed their support. Iris helped clean the kitchen area while Curtis spoke with other protesters. An impromptu meeting among the full group then convened in order to discuss the group's next step. By this time, there were more than a hundred people inside the barracks, including some children. The overwhelming consensus was that they should stay inside as long as possible. Most of the protesters lived in homes with no heat, no flush toilets, and no baths or showers. “Why should we leave? Where will we go? The base has stood empty for years. We're not taking anything from anyone.”

When the protesters first arrived at the base on Monday morning, there had been one Air Force officer and twenty-six civilian employees working there. After Lieutenant Colonel Andrews made his report to Washington, DC, two colonels, two majors, and a hundred and fifty Air Force police officers were flown into Greenville from Air Force bases across the country. On Tuesday, February 1, at 7:00 a.m., US Air Force Major General H. W. Puryear, the commanding general at Keesler Air Force Base in Biloxi, Mississippi, flew into Greenville to take command of the situation. Later that morning, at about 11:15, not long after Curtis and Iris arrived, Major General Puryear, along with a contingent of Air Force police, stood outside the barracks. He knocked on the door and said he wanted to discuss the situation. He was given permission to enter, and he did so by himself. Puryear told the group that they had to leave immediately, adding that they were creating a problem “in terms of a health and fire hazard.” He tried to assure them that “if you leave peacefully, I will see that your demands are presented in an official manner to whomever you designate,” even President Johnson.[9] Before turning to leave, he said he would give them twenty minutes to leave voluntarily and peacefully.

Once Puryear left, a discussion ensued among the occupiers. Iris and Curtis just listened: they were there as supporters, not decision-makers. The basic tenor of the discussion was that the federal government had been aware of their problems for over three years and failed to do anything to help them. Why expect any meaningful help now? They voted to stay put, with everyone remaining in the barracks.

At about 11:30 a.m., Air Force police in groups of four broke windows and knocked down doors to gain entrance into the barracks. They had been ordered, however, to not bring their nightsticks inside with them, so they left them in a pile outside the building before storming it.[10] When ordered to leave the base, about half of the protesters agreed to do so. The officers escorted them peacefully off the premises. The remaining members of the group, however, refused to budge, with most of them going limp and lying on the floor to make it more difficult for the police to extricate them. Most of them were nevertheless lifted by the Air Force police officers and dumped outside the base's gates. Some of the protesters refused to be carried out of the barracks peacefully and resisted their removal. They struggled and kicked, some of them biting the officers. A few of the protesters jumped on the backs of police officers. In the scuffle, the clothing of some of the officers and the protesters was torn, and some of the protesters sustained injuries as the officers dragged them across the floor and then across the lawn toward the gate. Some shouted profanities at the police officers. "Kick the hell out of them." Some yelled at the Black police officers, "Don't fight for the White folks,"[11] or addressed them as "Uncle Tom." A few of the officers were spat on.[12] Also shouted were anti–Vietnam War and antimilitary slogans. One protester fainted and had to be transported to a local doctor. Fortunately, no one was seriously injured.

Curtis offered no resistance as he was carried outside the base peacefully after he lay limp on the floor of the barracks. But not Iris. When a police officer came over to her as she lay limp on the floor, she refused to move. When he went to lift her, she screamed and kicked. Then Iris bit his leg. Eventually, when the police officer managed to get Iris off the floor, he flung her over his shoulder. She continued to scream and kick and then began biting the officer's shoulder. This continued all the way until the officer dumped Iris outside the base, not far from where Curtis was waiting for her. As she was telling Curtis that she had not been injured, several journalists came over to them. Iris recognized a few of them from when she and Curtis had entered the base. They asked her to describe what had happened inside the barracks, and she spoke with them for a few minutes about what she had experienced.

It took less than thirty minutes for the police to clear the barracks and move everyone off the base. No arrests were made, and no charges were ever filed against any of the organizers or the occupiers. Once everyone had been moved outside the gates, the group dispersed, with most of them walking back to the section of Greenville where they lived. Curtis and Iris drove back to Columbia.

That night, a press conference was held at the Greenville office of the Delta Ministry. Several people spoke.[13] Isaac Foster, a leader of an earlier plantation workers' strike, said it was important for poor people to form their own government. Unita Blackwell of the MFDP commented that the federal government had proven that it did not care about poor people; that the poor people of Mississippi were tired of getting nothing from the federal government; and that no one in the government represented them or their needs.[14] Ida Mae Lawrence of the Mississippi Freedom Labor Union complained that the federal government cared more about buildings than poor people: "Instead of getting what we was asking, we got the whole Air Force troopers in on us. The base is more thought of than the poor people. The buildings weren't doing anything but just sitting there. The building was more respectable than poor hungry people with nothing and nowhere to go." Rev. Arthur Thomas, director of the Delta Ministry of the National Council of Churches, blamed Secretary of Agriculture Orville Freeman and Attorney General Nicholas Katzenbach for acting in a "cruel and inhumane" manner. In response to questions asked by journalists, it was announced that there would not be another attempt to move into the abandoned Greenville barracks. The new plan was to persuade sharecroppers to leave the cotton plantations and move into a tent city on the outskirts of Greenville. About seventy-five sharecroppers eventually followed this plan.

Several newspapers published articles on the attempted Greenville Air Force Base takeover. One article described the protesters as "crazed, loud and dangerous" and the law enforcement officials and Air Force top brass as "merciful enough to forego filing charges."[15] *The New York Times* on February 1, 1966, ran an article with the headline "Mississippi Air Base Occupied by Negroes in Search of Jobs." The article mentioned the frigidly cold weather the area had experienced of late, the lack of jobs, food, and housing in the Delta, and the sincere desire of the occupiers for job training, quoting them as saying, "We are willing to work for ourselves if given a chance." The article also mentioned that Lieutenant Colonel Andrews claimed that one of the protesters had kicked him in the shin, and that journalists had not been allowed to enter the occupied building.[16] This article stopped there, as it had been written before the eviction of the occupiers. The next day, *The New York Times* ran another article that described the eviction. Written by journalist Gene Roberts, its headline declared: "Air Force Ejects Negroes Occupying a Mississippi Base."[17] The article mentioned by name three people who Roberts had been able to interview outside the gates. Mrs. Viola Hall, a fifty-nine-year-old woman from Wall, Mississippi, said she had survived the unusually harsh winter only by cutting and selling firewood, but she could no longer do such work, so she had come to the Air Force base. Booker Nelson, a displaced farm worker, was also quoted. And then the article mentioned "Miss Iris Eller [*sic*], a white woman from Philadelphia, who bit an airman on the leg."

Iris's father, Morris, happened to subscribe to *The New York Times*. When he saw the article, he strongly suspected that "Iris Eller" was none other than his daughter, Iris Geller. He had not been in touch with her since her return from Savannah, but he had surmised that she was somewhere in the South doing civil rights work. Even though Eva had been in communication with Iris (and Ira) while Iris was in Columbia, she had not discussed this with her husband. Apparently Morris did not know that Eva knew of Iris's exact whereabouts. After Morris quickly read through the rest of the paper, he threw it into the trash. Later that day, he received a telephone call from a friend from the postal workers' union. At the end of the conversation, his friend asked Morris whether his daughter was in Mississippi with civil rights protesters. The friend said he read an article in the *Times* that mentioned an "Iris Eller" from Philadelphia. Morris replied that he had seen the same article, but that it could not be his daughter, as she was attending classes at Temple University, and he had recently seen her at their home.

Back in Columbia, Iris and Curtis recounted their experience on the base to W.J. and Ira. Iris, half joking, said that she thought she was about to accomplish her goal of getting arrested when she kicked and bit the police officer. She had dreamed about being arrested while fighting for the movement, just like many others she knew and admired.[18] Ira cautioned her to abandon her dream of getting arrested, especially in Mississippi. He recounted his time in Mississippi jails. Although he doubted a White woman would be beaten and treated as poorly as he had been, a Mississippi jail was one place no one would ever want to be.

Meanwhile, in Washington, after receiving notice of the eviction of the occupiers at the Greenville base, Katzenbach met with President Johnson. He told the president that he had learned that the protesters did not plan to attempt a second takeover. Katzenbach warned the president, however, that the situation in Mississippi, as demonstrated by the events in Greenville, was "potentially explosive."[19] Katzenbach further told Johnson that thousands of poor Black workers in the Greenville area had lost jobs and homes, and that the local White leaders were unwilling to help them in any way. Federal funds that had been allocated for food assistance were not being distributed by local state officials, and neither were federal funds for employment training and Head Start programs for children. Katzenbach urged Johnson to authorize direct federal programs that would not rely on the involvement and cooperation of local officials, who had repeatedly shown that they were opposed to all federal programs to help the poor, especially poor Black people. Johnson agreed to the direct federal funding plan.

Over the next few months Greenville Air Force Base remained abandoned, although more heavily guarded. The occupation had gotten the attention of a great many people, including Dr. King. In response, King and the SCLC developed a plan to turn the airbase into a center for job training, housing, and other community support programs. He communicated directly with President Johnson about these plans, and Johnson agreed to support legislation to help achieve them. This proposed legislation, however, was killed by John Stennis, the US senator from Mississippi. As a member of the Senate Appropriations Committee, Stennis routinely used his position to block any legislation that sought to help poor Black people in Mississippi.[20] Later that year, in December 1966, the entire Air Force base was transferred to the control of the City of Greenville to be used as a commercial airport. Today it serves the area as the Mid Delta Regional Airport. Iris's involvement with the occupation at the Greenville Air Force Base was her proudest moment in the civil rights movement.

CHAPTER 11

Back to Philadelphia

AFTER HER EXPERIENCE AT GREENVILLE, Iris returned to her busy schedule with SNCC in Columbia. Her relationship with Curtis strengthened, and her relationship with her mother had at least stabilized, with weekly $10 bills and weekly telephone calls. Iris continued to say nothing to Eva about Curtis. Their conversations were cordial, but not forthcoming. Several months after Greenville, Iris began to think about returning to Philadelphia. It was not because of any dissatisfaction with her work in Columbia, or any conflict with Curtis, Ira, or W.J. It was just that she felt that her time with SNCC was coming to an end.

Throughout SNCC's existence, there had always been internal conflicts among its members and leaders about the role of Whites in the organization.[1] Although Whites had been part of SNCC since its beginning, the organization was founded on the belief that Black leadership was essential to achieving economic and political equality for Black people. By 1966 the Black Power movement had gained momentum.[2] During that summer, Stokely Carmichael took over from John Lewis as chairman of SNCC. Carmichael represented those within SNCC who believed that only Black workers could convey the message that Black people were capable of economic and political success through their own efforts. He believed that White supporters and workers were furthering white supremacy without realizing it. Carmichael said the "ultimate lie" was that Black people inherently could not achieve the same things without White help. "It must be the oppressed to whom SNCC addresses itself primarily, not to friends from the oppressing group."[3] He saw the need for "psychological equality" as a reason why

SNCC should rely solely on Black workers in Black communities. Using White workers in Black communities contradicted the goal of Black self-determination. In May 1966, at a meeting in Kingston Springs, Tennessee, SNCC leadership adopted a resolution that White members should only work in White communities.[4] The problem was that SNCC had no presence in White communities. The resolution was interpreted to mean that there was no longer any place for Whites in SNCC.

By the summer of 1966, the original SNCC principles based on religion and nonviolence had lost their relevance among the younger Black community. Black nationalism, Malcolm X, the Nation of Islam, and the Black Panther Party had more appeal to young Black people than interracial groups committed to long-term community organizing. Nonviolence made little sense when continually faced with police brutality aimed at the Black community. However, as SNCC moved towards a "Black Power" model, fundraising became more difficult. In 1966, the organization's finances were in bad shape. Many workers had not been paid their $10 weekly salary for months. The nonviolent, interracial nature of SNCC had been instrumental in getting northern White financial support. Such financial support was now disappearing.

The passage of the 1964 Civil Rights Act and the 1965 Voting Rights Act also changed the civil rights landscape. Many people who had worked for the major civil rights organizations decided that they could be more effective by working within the Democratic Party.[5] Others left to work for governmental and nongovernmental antipoverty programs begun under the aegis of President Johnson's Great Society legislation. SNCC lost many workers, especially the more moderate people with integrationist views. Carmichael spoke of what he perceived as the failures of an integrationist agenda. Integration did not address poverty. Integration only meant that those Black people who were successful now had the ability to leave their communities. The push for integration was based on "acceptance" that White society was superior. Integration "drained" the energy and skills from Black communities and transferred them to White neighborhoods. This growing view of Black Power, sometimes referred to as "Black militancy," had special attraction to younger Black people. At the same time, however, it alienated many White liberals. In June 1966, after the attempted murder in Mississippi of civil rights activist James Meredith,[6] the first Black to attend the University of Mississippi, Carmichael gave a well-publicized speech in Greenwood, Mississippi, where he spoke of the need for "Black Power," thus cementing the connection between SNCC and the Black Power movement.[7]

At a SNCC staff retreat in December 1966 at Peg Leg Bates Country Club in Kerhonkson, upstate New York, when a motion was introduced to exclude White members from voting at SNCC meetings, it became clear that SNCC had moved away from its "integrationist past."[8] Not long thereafter, in 1967, H. Rap Brown, an activist known for his Black nationalism, took over the leadership of SNCC. Soon SNCC joined with the Black Panther Party in openly advocating the right of Black people to armed self-defense. Most SNCC members had abandoned nonviolence well before then.[9] Similar organizations such as CORE also underwent change. At its 1965 convention, CORE abandoned its nonviolent tradition and now identified with the Black Power movement. Most of CORE's White members left the organization, as did James Farmer[10] and other original Black members who had been so committed to CORE's founding principles.

At the Nathan Street Freedom House in Columbia during the summer of 1966, Curtis, Iris, Ira, and W.J. discussed and debated at length the future of SNCC, the role of Whites in the civil rights movement, and the future of the movement in general. The discussions were intense, impassioned, and often lasted hours into the night. These discussions did not, however, influence their daily community activities in Columbia or their personal relationships, though all four of them realized that changes were inevitable. After much thought, Iris was the first to make a decision. She concluded that more progress for racial justice would be made if Whites left SNCC and Black people had total control. She now believed that White participation in SNCC, as well as in other civil rights organizations, was hurting the movement and holding back progress in achieving racial equality. She announced to the others that she was leaving Columbia and returning to Philadelphia. Ira, W.J., and especially Curtis wondered if Iris's decision was based not so much on her view of the role of Whites in SNCC as on her personal relationship with Curtis. Was she trying to get out of the relationship without personally rejecting him? Was she scared that a life with a Black man would be too difficult? Was she looking to move on to her next fling, whether personal or political? Iris insisted that she had based her decision solely on her conclusion that the time had come for her as a White person to leave SNCC. She was steadfast in this position in her discussions at the Freedom House. Many years later, she reiterated this position in her conversations with me when I presented the same arguments that she had heard in Columbia. She was not oblivious to the personal issue of leaving Curtis, but she had decided that whatever happened between herself and him would work itself out.

After her decision to leave Columbia, Iris spent a few weeks saying goodbye to those with whom she had worked. She told everyone she would be back to see them, but in fact she never returned. She thought she would see Ira again, probably in New York or Philadelphia. She doubted that she would see W.J. unless she returned to Columbia. As for Curtis, who knew? Their relationship was strong, but would it survive when they were living different lives and the physical distance between them was over a thousand miles? After all, Iris was going to be a college student in Philadelphia, and Curtis was staying as a worker for SNCC in Mississippi.

In August, Curtis drove Iris to the bus station in Hattiesburg. Not much was said during the drive. When it came time for Iris to board the bus to Atlanta, her first stop on the journey home to Philadelphia, Curtis and Iris embraced, their futures both as a couple and activists uncertain.

After Iris arrived in Philadelphia, she went back to the apartment where she had lived before leaving for Columbia. Her friend and roommate welcomed her back, especially since the woman who had been living in Iris's room had recently moved out. Iris then called her mother. She told Eva that she was back in Philadelphia and living in Powelton Village. She did not give the address, but said she would try to come by the house when she had a chance. She also told her mother to stop sending the weekly $10 bills to Columbia. Eva did not insist that Iris visit her or Morris, and the conversation was more informational than emotional. Iris felt that she had done her duty in telling her mother she was no longer in Columbia, but she felt no need to visit her parents. She remembered well the reception she had received upon returning home from Savannah, and she did not want to go through that again.

Iris contacted Temple University and asked to be readmitted for the upcoming fall semester. Although her resignation letter to Temple's president had been highly critical of the university, Temple readmitted her. No grades of F had gone on her academic record for having withdrawn from her courses late when she left with Curtis for Columbia. She obtained a part-time job with a City of Philadelphia welfare agency, making home visits and preparing reports on the condition of home environments, including the health and welfare of the occupants, especially children. For the first couple months, Iris and Curtis communicated through the mail. Their letters indicated that they missed one another very much, and that their relationship amounted to more than just a fling between two civil rights workers. Then they began to talk to each other by telephone on a regular basis. It was obvious from the tone of their conversations that a serious romantic relationship still existed.

Shortly after Iris left Columbia, she had learned from Curtis that Ira was planning to leave Columbia and SNCC. Ira had worked with SNCC for several years, and now he too decided that the time had come to move on. Although he would remain committed to racial equality and justice his entire life, his activism would be through other organizations. Curtis told Iris that W.J. had also decided to stop working full time for SNCC and planned to return to his job as a truck driver, hauling timber. This job did not pay much, but it was more than what SNCC had agreed to pay, which it recently had not been paying at all. Curtis now found himself the only one left at the Nathan Street Freedom House. He told Iris that he planned to stay in Columbia and continue the work they had done together, but he didn't know much longer he would stay there. He had been told by SNCC headquarters in Atlanta that it had no plans to send replacements for Ira and W.J.

In September Curtis visited his parents in Biloxi and told them that he was considering leaving SNCC and moving to Philadelphia, Pennsylvania, to be with a girl he had worked with in Columbia. She had returned to her hometown, he said, and was working with the city's welfare office and attending Temple University. His parents at first seemed pleased that he had met someone he was serious about, and might now "settle down." But when he told his parents that the girl was White, they reacted angrily. How could someone who had worked so hard for Black rights get involved with a White girl? They told him they were strongly against him going to Philadelphia, and that he would be destroying his life if he followed this White girl there. They asked if her parents knew about him, and he admitted that they didn't; Iris had in fact never mentioned him to her parents. Curtis's parents warned him that he would never be accepted by her family, and they would always treat him poorly. Was that how he wished to be treated? Was that the life he wanted? Upset by his parents' reaction, Curtis told them that he would go back to Columbia to think it over. Over the next few days, he thought about what he wanted to do, and what he should do. In the end, he decided to move to Philadelphia to be with Iris.

When Curtis called Iris to tell her the news, she was elated. It was not exactly a marriage proposal, but it was close to one. Both understood that marriage would probably not be possible in the short term. At the time, seventeen states had laws that made it a crime for a White and Black person to marry. Mississippi had such a law, as did all the other Southern states. Even states outside the Deep South, such as Delaware, Maryland, and West Virginia, all of which bordered Pennsylvania, prohibited mixed-race marriages. Pennsylvania, however, had no such prohibition, though interracial marriages were not common there.

Curtis requested and was granted an indefinite leave of absence from SNCC. Once he arrived in Philadelphia, he moved into the Powelton Village apartment with Iris. He took a job as a counselor at a local youth center, while Iris carried a full course load as a student in Temple University's social work program and continued to work part-time for the Philadelphia welfare office. In Philadelphia, the fear of being seen on the street as a mixed-race couple was not as great as in Mississippi, but nevertheless Iris and Curtis avoided any public displays of affection.

From the time that Iris returned to Philadelphia from Columbia, she continued to keep in touch with her mother by telephone every week. However, she did not talk with her father or visit her parents' home. Eva, and probably Morris, knew she was attending Temple University and living in an apartment in Powelton Village, but they had no idea that Curtis was living with her. For that matter, Iris's parents had no idea she was involved in a serious relationship with any man, much less a Black man. During spring break in 1967, Iris and

Curtis began to discuss marriage. At the time, a case was pending in the US Supreme Court challenging the Virginia law that criminalized mixed-race marriages. This case, *Loving v. Virginia*,[11] led to greater awareness and focus nationally on mixed-race relationships and marriages. A Supreme Court decision invalidating Virginia's prohibition of mixed-race marriages would apply to all states and certainly help, they believed, lead to wider acceptance of relationships such as theirs. On June 12, 1967, the court unanimously declared Virginia's statute as unconstitutional. Now mixed-race marriages were legal in the entire country.

In response to the decision in *Loving*, Iris and Curtis decided to get married. Although uncertain over whether to do so, Iris decided to tell her mother about Curtis. This was not a discussion that she looked forward to having. When Iris told her mother that she had been seriously involved with a man from the time she was in Mississippi, and that the two of them had decided to get married, Eva, assuming the man was Ira, seemed pleased. But when Iris told her that the man she planned to marry was a Black man named Curtis, the line went silent. After what seemed forever to Iris, Eva then asked her if she was sure she knew what she was doing. Did she really want to ruin her life by marrying a Black man? Iris responded that she was certain about what she wanted and would be doing. She was not asking for permission or approval; she simply wanted to have the courtesy to inform her parents before she got married. The conversation ended with Eva wishing Iris good luck, but making no plans to meet Curtis or see Iris anytime soon. Iris felt the call had gone about as well as she could have expected. At least her mother had not screamed and threatened to have Curtis arrested. The next day, Iris got a call from Eva, who told her that her father, Morris, had one request. All marriage license applications filed in Philadelphia City Hall were published in the daily Philadelphia newspapers, *The Philadelphia Inquirer* and *The Evening Bulletin*. Although the races of the applicants were not mentioned, Morris did not want the notice of Iris's and Curtis's marriage license published. He was afraid that relatives, friends, and co-workers would, upon reading that Iris planned to wed, ask him about it, and he did not wish to discuss the matter with anyone. He requested, therefore, that Iris obtain a marriage license in Chester County, just south of Philadelphia, so that no notice of the marriage license application would appear in a Philadelphia paper. Rather than escalate the tensions with her parents, Iris agreed to do so. A few days later, she and Curtis obtained their Pennsylvania marriage license in Chester County. No one in the family or among the family's friends knew of Iris's marriage, which took place at the Chester County courthouse in June 1967.

After their marriage, Iris and Curtis continued to live in the same Powelton Village apartment. Now Curtis took a job at a minimum-security prison, working mostly with young Black first-time offenders. He developed close relationships with the young men he tried to help, teaching them how to improve their reading skills (or in some cases how to read) by assigning and discussing books by Black authors such as W. E. B. Du Bois, Frederick Douglass, and Malcolm X. After several months, however, prison officials told Curtis that they did not approve of his methods of counseling or choice of assigned reading. They ordered him instead to follow what they described as "traditional established" social work principles. When Curtis refused to change his approach with the youthful prisoners, he was fired. After this experience, Curtis never returned to social work or counseling. Instead he got work as a truck driver, a job he stayed with for over two decades. Nor did he ever again become actively involved in any civil rights organization or the civil rights movement.

Iris, meanwhile, continued her studies at Temple University. In early 1968, she and Curtis became parents to a baby girl. They said nothing about the baby to Eva, Morris, or any other family member. Iris became involved with a group of mothers of infants and young children at Temple. The group successfully lobbied the university to open a day-care center for students with young children. After Iris graduated from Temple with a degree in social work, she got a job as a probation officer. After a couple years, she worked with the local welfare office.

The marriage between Iris and Curtis ended in divorce in 1971, about four years after they married. Their divorce had nothing to do with any racial or political differences, or pressure from either family. Both agreed that Iris should be granted legal custody of their daughter. Curtis stayed in Philadelphia and continued his work as a truck driver. He remarried; his second wife was also a White Jewish social worker.[12] Iris remarried, too. Her second husband was a White man who over the years owned several small businesses. She had a son with her second husband, and the couple lived mostly in the Philadelphia area, but also for a few years in Raleigh, North Carolina.

After her divorce from Curtis, Iris reached out to her parents. She had not seen them for about six years. Although her parents knew that she had married a Black man with the first name of Curtis, they never met him; nor did they know that Iris had a child with him. Iris explained to her parents that she had obtained a divorce and then told them about her daughter, who was now three years old. The sharing of the news of the divorce and the child was the first step in Iris's attempt to mend her relationship with her parents. She was also interested in seeing other family members, her aunts, uncles, and cousins. She had not seen any extended family members in almost seven years. During all this time, Eva and Morris had not discussed Iris with anyone. The unwritten agreement among the family not to ask about Iris or even mention her name had never been broken. Iris asked her mother whether it would now create any problems if she were to get together with family members and attend family functions. The answer was that this would not be a problem. Iris then asked if it would create any problems if she brought her daughter to these family functions. Again, she was told that this would not pose a problem.

When Iris returned to family events after being gone for almost seven years, there was no welcome-back party, and no celebration of the birth of her daughter. It was more as if she had never been gone, and nothing unusual had happened. No one asked questions such as "Where have you been?" "What have you been doing?" "Who is the father of this little girl?" "Did you adopt this little Black girl?"—though undoubtedly all these questions were in the minds of family members when they first saw Iris after all those years. Equally strange was that Iris never discussed anything about the years she had been away. She too acted as if nothing out of the ordinary had occurred. When Morris died, nothing changed. When Eva died, almost thirty years after Iris's return to the family with her daughter, nothing changed. Moreover, Iris never seemed offended or disappointed that no one had ever asked where she had been or what she had done. Her story remained unasked and untold.

EPILOGUE

AS I WROTE IN THE introduction to this book, when I finally asked Iris about her possible involvement in the civil rights movement, she was pleased at my request, writing "I am quite moved." Once I asked, she was happy to share her story. Because no one ever asked whether she had a story to tell, perhaps Iris felt that no one cared where she had been, what she had been doing, or who was the father of her daughter. Throughout the many years before I started my research, I had assumed the opposite: that she had no desire to talk about those years because she did not want to open closed wounds. Maybe she felt guilty about how she had upset her parents. Perhaps she was disappointed in herself that she had shut off communications with her cousins. As for Eva and Morris, I now believe that their major concern from the beginning of Iris's interest in joining the civil rights movement was their daughter's safety. They honestly feared that she would be killed in the South. They also wanted her to graduate from college, something only one member of the entire extended family at that time had accomplished. Education was the most important avenue to success for first-generation Americans. I also think that Eva and Morris were embarrassed by their loss of control over their daughter and what could be seen as her loss of respect for them. Did racism play any role in their reactions? I do not think one can dismiss that.

Iris and I met on numerous occasions at her apartment in Philadelphia to discuss those events that had taken place over fifty years earlier. At the time we met, she was seventy years old and had just retired as a social worker. She had worked mostly in the public sector for different welfare agencies. Throughout the years, she supported liberal causes, organizations, and candidates. Although in subsequent years she never devoted herself to civil rights activism as she had as a young college student, her belief in the need to fight for racial equality and justice never lessened. Iris's idealism never waned, and throughout her entire adult life, she strongly believed that change would occur through the actions of everyday people. She never regretted the sacrifices she made or her lack of measurable success in achieving the goals she had strived for. Iris periodically considered running for local political office, but she never took the next step. She found personal fulfillment through her work as a social worker and her renewed relationship with her immediate and extended family which now included her daughter.

When I began my discussions with Iris, she and her husband had recently moved back to Philadelphia from Raleigh, North Carolina, where they had lived for the past several years. Her husband was not in good health and had sold his copy center business just prior to their move. As I was coming to the end of my career as a full-time law professor, I was looking to become involved in a project to keep myself busy once I stopped teaching. At our first meeting, I explained that I was interested in her story as a long-standing member of academia, not as a family member. My goal was to write a historical narrative of the civil rights movement from a perspective that was different from other books, not a "kiss and tell" book or one that tried to explain family dynamics. I told her of my commitment to confidentiality based on my training and career as an attorney.

During our meetings, Iris remembered many of the events in which she had participated in detail and with emotion. She teared up occasionally when talking about her experiences.[1] She seemed excited to share her story with me. There were many parts of her story, however, that she could not recall, especially names. I was able to fill in missing pieces by meeting in person with Boyd Faust,[2] Ira Grupper,[3] and Michael Simmons.[4] Curtis had died twenty years earlier. Other facts I gathered through books,[5] newspaper articles, and websites. I traveled to Columbia, Mississippi, and spoke with people there. I saw buildings Iris had spoken about. The Freedom House on Nathan Street has been torn down, but I visited the empty lot. The movie theater still stands, but no longer has a segregated balcony. Older residents remembered it. The Lampton's building is no longer a department store, but the building still says "Lampton's." I remember calling Iris and saying, "You won't believe where I am now," just before I sent her pictures from Columbia through my cell phone. She had never returned to Columbia since she left in 1966.

My plan was to meet in person with Iris after I had engaged in my own research, and to tell her what I had learned from other sources, people, and my travel to see if any of it refreshed her memory. When I tried to reconnect with her, she did not return my emails or telephone messages. A few months after not hearing anything, I learned from her daughter, with whom I had kept in touch over the years, that Iris and her husband had moved out of the apartment in Philadelphia where I had conducted my interviews with her. Her daughter also told me that Iris had been recently diagnosed with Alzheimer's disease. Although her diagnosis came after our in-person interviews had concluded, looking back, she had undoubtedly been experiencing some Alzheimer's-related issues from the beginning of our discussions.

I learned that Iris had been moved to a memory care unit in a health care facility in Philadelphia, while her husband lived in an assisted living section of the same facility. This was shortly before the Covid-19 pandemic began. In early winter 2020 I made plans to visit her, giving proper notice to the nurses and other staff. This time her cognitive abilities were much worse than when we last spoke about one year earlier. She remembered me and my wife, who had accompanied me to the hospital, but spoke of events that I know never occurred. She had some bizarre stories about her parents. She did remember a few things from her civil rights worker days, especially biting the police officer at Greenville Air Force Base, but she no longer had the ability to share her story. I realized that had I waited any longer to ask Iris whether she had a story to tell about her time as a civil rights worker, that story, and perhaps the stories of some others in this book,[6] would have remained forever untold.

During one of our earlier meetings, Iris had described herself as a "nobody" in the civil rights movement. She was clearly not a leader, and her name does not appear in any of the histories of the movement. But that hardly means she was a nobody. Moreover, there were a great many civil rights workers like Iris who did their best to effect change, who uprooted their lives to do so, and who never tried to take any credit for it. In 2013 Duke University entered a partnership with the SNCC Legacy Project to serve as a resource for the study of the civil rights movement in the 1960s. Its website contains the following statement: "Most histories of the Civil Rights Movement focus on the great leaders, dramatic marches and legislative changes that dominated the headlines. By contrast, [we] will examine the behind-the-scenes work, circumstances and coalitions that shifted the national agenda toward voting rights."[7] In 2016 Bernie Sanders was running for the Democratic Party nomination for president against Hillary Clinton. John Lewis, then a congressman, supported Clinton. At one point during the campaign, Sanders spoke of his involvement in the civil rights movement in the 1960s when he was a student at the University of Chicago. Sanders had been a member of SNCC and CORE, and had been arrested during a protest against segregation. Initially, Lewis commented regarding Sanders, "I never saw him. I never met him." After some criticism for this comment, Lewis felt compelled to add at a later date, "The fact that I did not meet him does not mean I doubted that Senator Sanders participated. Thousands sacrificed in the 1960s whose names we will never know, and I have always given honor to their contribution."[8] We know the names Martin, John, Malcolm, Hosea, and Stokely. What about Boyd, Ira, Curtis, and W.J.? What about Iris? The well-known leaders of the civil rights movement of the 1960s deserve all the attention and praise that they have gotten. But to those whose stories remain untold and whose names have gone unspoken, I hope this book brings honor.

ACKNOWLEDGMENTS

THIS BOOK WOULD NEVER HAVE come to fruition without the involvement of several people who I recognize with gratitude here. First, my wife Ria. From the time she first met members of my extended family, she urged me to inquire about the mystery of my cousin Iris's disappearance in the mid 1960's. My response was usually some cliché such as "let sleeping dogs lie," or "I'm not going to open Pandora's Box." Eventually, however, I agreed with her that I should try to learn whether an important story lurked behind years of silence. This led me to meet and interview courageous people who had committed themselves to racial justice and equality during the 1960s. Once I realized that there might be a story worth telling, I received encouragement from many people to continue my efforts. They too wanted to know the full story. Special among these early supporters were Jim Wharton, a family friend, and Cassandra Havard, a colleague and friend. When I told them what I was working on, they both were so interested in my project that I did not want to disappoint them by abandoning my plan. There were other colleagues, friends, and casual acquaintances with whom I shared my new project. I had recently retired from full-time law school teaching so the typical question asked of me was "what do you do now with your time?" When I told them of my possible book, I received further encouragement. "That sounds interesting." "I can't wait to read the book." I was never certain whether their enthusiasm for the story was genuine or they were merely being polite, but it kept me going, and I thank them, too numerous to name here.

Family members such as my brother Earl, sister-in-law Deena, and cousins Bruce Goldin and Tara Styles, provided validation of my efforts by expressing their excitement when I told them of what I was learning through my research. They too had wondered about Iris, but now I was engaged in unearthing things they thought they would never learn. Even the emails and telephone calls that merely asked "how's the book coming" meant a lot to me, and I thank them.

While writing earlier drafts of the manuscripts, two long-time friends, Cynthia Chambers and Steven Grossman, offered feedback on both substance and style. It was important to me to learn how others were reacting to what I was writing. Based on their comments, the manuscript went through numerous changes. Their input was invaluable, and I greatly appreciate the time and effort they spent on my behalf.

At this stage of my professional career, I want to recognize three men who provided me with opportunities when I was a very young lawyer that allowed me to pursue my career as a lawyer, law professor, and author. David Ginsburg and Thomas C. Green were lawyers in Washington, D.C., who hired me to work with them on the Watergate case. I do not have the words to express how grateful I am to these two famous lawyers who taught me what it means to be a lawyer. Next, Laurence M. Katz was the Dean at the University of Baltimore School of Law who hired me at the age of twenty-seven to join the full-time faculty. Larry supported my teaching and scholarship throughout his service as dean, and I want to recognize him here.

I will end these acknowledgments by thanking many others who are not named but who deserve my thanks for their contribution to this book and my career. Be assured that they too have a special place in my heart.

NOTES

Introduction

1. Robert Mardian served as assistant attorney general for internal security under attorney general John Mitchell during the first term of Richard Nixon's presidency. At the Watergate trial before Judge John Sirica, Mardian was convicted of conspiracy to obstruct justice along with Mitchell and Nixon White House advisers John Ehrlichman and H. R. Haldeman. On appeal, Mardian presented several arguments why his conviction should be overturned, including the insufficiency of the evidence, the admission into evidence of the White House tapes, and errors in the jury instructions. Although I did not participate in any of the legal work at trial, I was a member of the legal team that prepared Mardian's appeal. The US Court of Appeals for the District of Columbia Circuit unanimously reversed Mardian's conviction on the ground that he should have been tried in a separate trial apart from the others. *United States v. Mardian*, 546 F.2d 973 (D.C. Cir. 1976). The Watergate special prosecutor eventually dropped all charges against Mardian.

2. Rochvarg, *Watergate Victory*.

3. See, for example, "Watergate, Multiple Conspiracies, and the White House Tapes," 16 Chapman L. Rev. 47 (2012); and "Enron, Watergate and the Regulation of the Legal Profession," 43 Washburn L. Rev. 601 (2003).

4. Dean was White House Counsel during President Nixon's presidency, and was personally involved in many of the events constituting the Watergate scandal. He wrote a best-selling book, *Blind Ambition*, about Watergate. His testimony before the Senate Select Committee on Watergate led to the resignation from office of President Nixon. His testimony at the Watergate conspiracy trial was instrumental to the convictions of John Mitchell, John Ehrlichman, and H. R. Haldeman. More recently, Dean has been a guest on television news programs and written several books on US history and politics.

5. These attempts at erasure are nothing new. See Carmichael and Thelwell, *Ready for Revolution*, 378n*, where it is noted that the policy of the school board in Bolivar County, Mississippi, was to prohibit public school American history courses from covering the period 1860 to 1875—the years of Reconstruction, when Blacks enjoyed some political rights and power.

Chapter 1

1. For a short discussion of the history of the racial composition of Northeast Philadelphia, see Matthew Smolarz, "Northeast Philadelphia," Encyclopedia of Greater Philadelphia, https://philadelphiaencyclopedia.org/essays/northeast-philadelphia-essay/. See also Meyers, *Oxford Circle*.

2. Northeast High School was the subject of a documentary film in 1968 by the critically acclaimed filmmaker Frederick Wiseman. The film's portrayal of students, teachers, and administrators was so controversial that the film was not shown in Philadelphia for many years because of concern over lawsuits. It is now considered to be a classic film about the 1960s, and was selected in 1991 for preservation in the National Film Registry. The author of this book appears in the movie for a very short time (thankfully). Although filmed several years after Iris had graduated, the movie accurately captures life at the school and the area during the entire decade in its emphasis on conformity and authority. Northeast High School also was the location of a reality television show, *Teach*, starring actor Tony Danza (David A. Hiller, dir.; aired on A&E, 2009–10) who taught actual classes. This show lasted only seven episodes. Unlike Wiseman's documentary, Danza's show never received any honors.

3. This was before casino gambling was legalized in Atlantic City. Once gambling came to Atlantic City, vacation destinations of families from the Northeast tended to shift to Margate, Ventnor, and other New Jersey beach towns.

4. Among those discussed as possible vice presidential candidates were Senators Hubert Humphrey of Minnesota, Abraham Ribicoff of Rhode Island, Thomas Dodd of Connecticut, and Eugene McCarthy of Wisconsin; Secretary of Defense Robert McNamara; and Governor Pat Brown of California.

5. Until 1950 contestants in the Miss America Pageant were restricted to those of "good health and of the white race." See "Breaking the Color Line," American Experience, PBS, last modified April 7, 2025, https://www.pbs.org/wgbh/americanexperience/features/missamerica-breaking-color-line/. Not until 1984 was a Black woman, Vanessa Williams, crowned Miss America. In the early 1960s the Miss America Pageant was the highest-rated television program in America. A few weeks after the 1964 Democratic National Convention, Miss Arizona, Vonda Kay Van Dyke, was crowned Miss America 1965. Her victory was based in no small part on her high score in the talent

portion of the competition. Van Dyke performed as a ventriloquist with a dummy.

6. There are many books that discuss Freedom Summer. One of the most well respected is Bruce Watson, *Freedom Summer*. Other useful books to understand Freedom Summer include Belfrage, *Freedom Summer*; McAdam, *Freedom Summer*; and Cagin, *We Are Not Afraid*. Freedom Summer was also the basis of the 1988 Hollywood movie *Mississippi Burning*, directed by Alan Parker (Burbank, CA: Warner Bros.). Although well received by the moviegoing public, the movie created controversy: many civil rights leaders, including Coretta Scott King, widow of Martin Luther King Jr., boycotted it because of its inaccurate portrayal of many events. In light of such criticism, the producers admitted to "artistic license," and the movie was eventually described as a "fictional" account of the murders of Goodman, Schwerner, and Chaney. See Toplin, *History by Hollywood*, 26–27.

7. See Oppenheimer, "Mobs, Vigilantes, Cops, and Feds."

8. Lawrence Bush, "Mississippi Freedom Summer—Fifty Years Later, Part One," *Jewish Currents*, Spring 2014, https://web.archive.org/web/20140625052028/https://jewishcurrents.org/mississippi-freedom-summer-fifty-years-later-part-one-28058.

9. Watson, *Freedom Summer*, 80.

10. See Brooks and Horick, *Speeches*.

11. See Joseph, *Stokely*, 76.

12. Tom Wicker, "Mississippi Delegates Withdraw, Rejecting a Seating Compromise," *New York Times*, August 26, 1964.

13. Among the reasons for the MFDP rejection of the offer was that the two MFDP delegates were to be selected by Democratic Party officials, not MFDP members, and that by sitting the all-White delegates from the regular Mississippi delegation, the convention would be acknowledging the legitimacy of the racist delegation from Mississippi. "Mississippi Freedom Democratic Party Congressional Challenge," Online Archive of California, https://oac.cdlib.org/view?docId=kt1v19n5bh;NAAN=13030&doc.view=frames&chunk.id=d0e260.

14. See discussion in Bond, "SNCC: What We Did." See also, generally, Lewis, *Walking with the Wind*.

15. See Holsaert et al., *Hands on the Freedom Plow*.

16. "MFDP Freedom Vote," SNCC Digital Gateway, https://www.snccdigital.org/events/mfdp-freedom-vote/. See also "Negroes Holding a Mock Election in Mississippi," *New York Times*, November 1, 1964. Bob Moses, a SNCC official, once said: "We (MFDP) hold mock elections, while the State of Mississippi holds mockeries of elections." "Mississippi Freedom Democratic Party Congressional Challenge," Online Archive of California.

17. "MFDP Freedom Vote."

18. "Mississippi Freedom Democratic Party Congressional Challenge," Online Archive of California. See also Dittmer, *Local People*; and Holsaert et al., *Hands on the Freedom Plow*, 230–39.

19. See "MFDP Freedom Vote." Representative William Ryan, a Democrat from New York, planned to propose a resolution that would hold vacant five seats that had been won by Mississippi Democrats until after the House of Representatives Committee on Administration heard and decided the challenge. Before Ryan could offer his proposal, Representative Carl Albert of Oklahoma, the House Democratic Party majority leader, was recognized by Speaker of the House Mike McCormack to offer a motion to seat the five White men from Mississippi. Albert's resolution passed 276 to 148, thus mooting Ryan's planned resolution. "Mississippi Freedom Democratic Party Congressional Challenge," Online Archive of California.

Chapter 2

1. Simmon's personal website is www.msimmons.org. Another website that discusses Simmon's activism is https://raday.blogs.com. Simmons is also discussed in Wallach and Kirk, *Arsnick*. See also Michael Simmons, "Arkansas Roots and Consciousness," 2009, Civil Rights Movement Archive (hereafter CRMA), https://www.crmvet.org/nars/simmons2.htm.

2. Between 1965 and 1971, sixty-four former students from Edison High School died in service in the Vietnam War. More from Edison High School died than from any other high school in the entire country.

3. An internet search will find many articles about Simmons and his many years of activism on behalf of numerous human rights issues, ranging from Black people in the United States to the Roma in Europe.

4. There is a short article and several pictures of the march organized by Conscience in the Temple University yearbook, *Templar*, 1965, https://www.e-yearbook.com/sp/eybb?school=10&year=1965.

5. The information set forth in the next few pages was obtained from several sources. The most useful source is Leventhal, *SCOPE of Freedom*, 51–54. Leventhal's book reproduces many original documents, including internal SCOPE memoranda, press releases, newspaper articles, and other primary sources relating to SCOPE. Most of the documents reproduced in Leventhal are also available in posts by civil rights veterans on the Civil Rights Movement Archive, www.crmvet.org.

6. Southern Christian Leadership Conference (hereafter SCLC), "SCLC SCOPE Project," 1965, CRMA, https://www.crmvet.org/docs/65_scope_brochure.pdf.

7. SCLC, "Meet Tommy Smith," SCOPE brochure, 1965, CRMA, https://www.crmvet.org/docs/65_scope_tommy.pdf.

8. SCLC, "SCLC SCOPE Project."

9. SCLC, "The Summer Community Organization and Political Education Project of the Southern Christian Leadership Conference," 1965, CRMA, https://www.crmvet.org/docs/65_sclc_scope.pdf. Reproduced in Leventhal, *SCOPE of Freedom*, 53–54. See also Gitin, *This Bright Light of Ours*, 23–24.

10. See "SCLC Spokesman to Outline Student Participation Roles," *The Heights*, May 7, 1965, https://newspapers.bc.edu/?a=d&d=bcheights19650507.2.21l; and Ellen Lake, "Civil Rights Groups Organize Separate Projects for Summer," *Harvard Crimson*, April 29, 1965, https://www.thecrimson.com/article/1965/4/29/civil-rights-groups-organize-separate-projects/.

11. SCLC, "Recruiting," 1965, in Leventhal, *SCOPE of Freedom*, 168–69, https://www.crmvet.org/docs/65_scope_recruiting.pdf.

12. SCLC, "Southern Community Organization."

13. Medical Committee for Human Rights to SCOPE Volunteers, May 25, 1965, CRMA, https://www.crmvet.org/docs/scope_mchr65.pdf.

14. SCLC, SCOPE project release form, 1965, CRMA, https://www.crmvet.org/docs/65_scope_release.pdf.

15. SCLC, "*Recruiting*." See also Gitin, *This Bright Light of Ours*, 22.

16. SCLC, "Preparatory Reading List for SCOPE Volunteers," summer 1965, CRMA, https://www.crmvet.org/docs/6506_scope_readinglist.pdf. Five books were required: *The Souls of Black Folk* by W. E. B. Du Bois; *Freedom Road* by Howard Fast; *Southern Politics in State and Nation* by V. O. Key Jr.; *The People That Walk in Darkness* by J. W. Schulte Nordholt; and *How to Win*, a handbook on political organization and voter registration prepared by the AFL-CIO Committee on Political Education. The "strongly recommended" readings were *The Mind of the South* by W. J. Cash; *Black Reconstruction* by W. E. B. Du Bois; *The Other America* by Michael Harrington; *Discrimination* by Wallace Mendelson; *The Movement* by Lorraine Hansberry; *Killers of the Dream* by Lillian Smith; *Strength to Love* by Martin Luther King Jr.; and *Black Boy* by Richard Wright. The listed "supplementary readings" were *The Strange Career of Jim Crow* by C. Vann Woodward; *The Negro Revolt* by Louis E. Loma; *The Negro Politician* by Edward T. Clayton; *The Negro in America* by Arnold Rose; *The Southern Heritage* by James McBride Dabbs; *Before the Mayflower* by Lerone Bennett; *Life and Writing of Frederick Douglass*, edited by Philip Foner; *Blues for Mister Charlie* by James Baldwin; *Fire Next Time* by James Baldwin; and *Freedom Ride* by James Peck.

17. See Dana Swan, "Selma Plus Thirty Years: A Personal Remembrance," in Leventhal, *SCOPE of Freedom*, 233–36.

18. Eig, *King*, 366–70.

19. SCLC, SCOPE project release form.

20. In *This Bright Light of Ours*, Maria Gitin discusses that when she asked her parents to sign the consent form, she told them that if they refused, she would forge their signatures. They signed. Gitin, *This Bright Light of Ours*, 22.

21. This was a typical requirement for women in the movement. See Joseph, *Stokely*, 70.

Chapter 3

1. See Rev. Dr. Janet Wolfe, "Letter to Campus Pastor about SCOPE Orientation Week," June 14–19, 1965, CRMA, https://www.crmvet.org/lets/6506wolf.htm. Wolfe's post presents an excellent, detailed discussion of the SCOPE orientation.

2. The lyrics to many of the songs of the civil rights movement can be found in "Freedom Song Sheet," CRMA, www.crmvet.org/docs/song_sheet.pdf.

3. Wolfe, "Letter to Campus Pastor."

4. Leventhal, *SCOPE of Freedom*, 149–51.

5. *Brown v. Board of Education*, 347 U.S. 483 (1954).

6. Wolfe, "Letter to Campus Pastor."

7. Lewis, *King*, 302.

8. See University of San Diego News Center, "Inside USD: Civil Rights Movement Inspired USD's Nelson," February 9, 2013, https://www.sandiego.edu/news/cas/detail.php?_focus=44164. Nelson was able to shake King's hand.

9. Title I covered voting rights: Local rules for voting needed to be equal for everyone. Title II concerned public accommodations such as motels, restaurants, movie theaters, and gasoline stations. Title III dealt with public housing. Title IV authorized the US attorney general and the Department of Health, Education and Welfare to bring actions in federal court to challenge local school segregation. The Civil Rights Commission was established by Title V, while Title VII created the Fair Employment Practices Commission. Title VI provided that no federal funds could be used in any activity that resulted in discrimination or segregation. Rauh commented that this section would be useful to attack school district gerrymandering and so-called freedom of choice plans that gave public funds to nonpublic schools. Under Title X, "Community Relations Services Under Department of Commerce," Rauh advised that this section could be used as a check on agricultural extension services to see if crop allotments had been discriminatorily manipulated.

10. Wolfe, "Letter to Campus Pastor."

11. See Paul Good, "600 Students Preach Rights Gospel in the South," *Washington Post*, July 12, 1965. Good writes that sexual relations between Black people and Whites were "definitely discouraged," and that all workers were instructed to "dress and behave courteously." It was also important that the student workers "escape the beatnik label."

12. See Joseph, *Stokely*, 70. "Carmichael warned against profanity, excessive drinking, and overt interracial dating. He advised against women wearing pants so as not to offend locals, and he set a 5p.m. standard curfew for returning to their living quarters."

13. See Tyson, *Blood of Emmett Till*.

14. SCLC, "What You Need to Do," SCOPE project brochure, 1965, CRMA, https://www.crmvet.org/docs/scope1.pdf.

15. See McAtee, *Transformed*, 82. The movie *Freedom Song*, directed by Phil Alden Robinson (Burbank, CA: TNT, 2000), starring Danny Glover, is a fictional account of racial violence in a small Mississippi town based on true events of racial violence in McComb. See also "Freedom Song," Zinn Education Project, https://www.zinnedproject.org/materials/freedom-song.

16. See Holsaert et al., *Hands on the Freedom Plow*, pt. 5.

17. See Willie Bolden, interview by Bob Short, October 7, 2009, Reflections on Georgia Politics Oral History Collection, ROGP 088, Richard B. Russell Library for Political Research and Studies, University of Georgia, https://ohms.libs.uga.edu/viewer.php?cachefile=russell/RBRL220ROGP-088.xml.

18. Benjamin Van Clark, "Siege at Savannah," *Freedomways*, 1st quarter, 1964. Reproduced in CRMA, https://www.crmvet.org/info/savanah1.htm.

19. Bruce Hartford, "Civil Rights Movement History 1965: Selma & the March to Montgomery," CRMA, https://www.crmvet.org/tim/timhis65.htm; and Dittmer, *The Good Doctors*.

20. In Rice, *Hosea Williams*, 126, the reason stated for King's absence from the march was that his father, Rev. Martin Luther King Sr. ("Daddy King") was ill and unable to preach, and King Jr. was needed at the Ebenezer Church in Atlanta.

21. Rice, 128; and Andrew Young, foreword to Rice, xi.

22. Hartford, "Civil Rights Movement History"*; and* Rice, *Hosea Williams*, 131–32.

23. Hartford, "Civil Rights Movement History."

24. Rice, *Hosea Williams*, 132.

25. *Williams v. Wallace*, 240 F. Supp. 100 (M.D. Ala., 1965).

26. This should be compared to SNCC's James Foreman and women members of SNCC, where women were not expected to be the cleaners. See Holsaert et al., *Hands on the Freedom Plow*, 340. Hosea Williams recalled, "I had a bunch of upper-class white folks and some priests and nuns that I gave the shittiest jobs to—the worse jobs of the march, taking care of the sanitary facilities and emptying slop buckets and garbage cans." Rice, *Hosea Williams*, 138.

Chapter 4

1. A handwritten letter by a White female SCOPE volunteer during her time in Luverne, Alabama, during the summer of 1965 was sold on eBay for $192.49 on February 17, 2015. "Life down here is entirely different from anything I've known before," the volunteer writes. "We are feared and suspected by the white community as being communists, n—r lovers, and northern

agitators." The author of the letter was deceased at the time of auction. The letter is no longer available on the eBay website, but the author has a copy of the listing that shows the letter.

2. For a discussion of the paper industry in Savannah and the impact it had on the community, see Reed, "Smells Like Money."

3. For a discussion by another civil rights worker on being Jewish and attending Sunday services at a Black church in the South, see Preacely, "It Was Simply in My Blood." More can be found at Peggy Trotter Dammond Preacely, www.peggytrotterdammondpreacely.com..

4. Hankerson had worked in Selma with Hosea Williams. He had also been one of the speakers at the SCOPE orientation in Atlanta on a panel that discussed voter registration techniques. His presentation is reproduced in Leventhal, *SCOPE of Freedom*, 361–62. Iris recognized him from orientation but did not recall any details of his presentation when she saw him in Savannah. Before becoming a full-time worker for SCLC, Hankerson had worked on the docks of Savannah. He had also served time in jail. Leventhal, 349.

5. Alter, *His Very Best.*

6. Hosea L. Williams, memorandum to SCOPE workers, July 1965, CRMA, https://www.crmvet.org/docs/65_scope_memo1.pdf.

7. *Harper v. Virginia Board of Elections*, 383 U.S. 663 (1966).

8. Strained relations between parents and those that volunteered for SCOPE were not unique to Iris and Boyd. See Gitin, *This Bright Light of Ours*, 175.

9. Ralph D. Abernathy, SCLC press statement, July 1, 1965, CRMA, https://www.crmvet.org/docs/650701_abernathy.pdf.

10. SCLC, "SCOPE/SCLC Incident Reports," 1965, CRMA, https://www.crmvet.org/docs/scopeinc.htm. Reproduced in Leventhal, *SCOPE of Freedom*, 367–84.

11. See Rice, *Hosea Williams*, 145–46.

Chapter 5

1. Americus-Sumter County Movement Remembered Committee, http://theamericusmovement.org/. A civil rights museum has been under consideration for many years in Americus. The mission of the proposed museum is to commemorate the civil rights activities in Americus in the 1960s. The museum has acquired the actual cell in which Dr. King was held for eventual display; it was dismantled and put in storage until the museum has a permanent location.

2. Americus-Sumter Committee.

3. Americus-Sumter Committee.

4. Americus-Sumter Committee.

5. Franklin, *Young Crusaders*, 84–85.

6. Americus-Sumter Committee.

7. Iris remembered the pet pig's name, but not the names of any family members with whom she stayed.

8. Franklin, *Young Crusaders*, 84–85.

9. "March Staged by 800 Persons in Americus," in Leventhal, *SCOPE of Freedom*, 493.

10. "Incidents, Demonstrations, etc.," in Leventhal, 370.

11. Eig, *King*, 293–97.

12. Hosea Williams, press release, July 26, 1965, in Leventhal, *SCOPE of Freedom*, 180–90.

13. "Americus Plans Bi-Racial Panel" and "Protests Stopped in Sumter County," in Leventhal, 502, 501.

14. "Rights Groups Rebuffed at 2 Americus Churches," *Los Angeles Times*, August 2, 1965, in Leventhal, 496–97; and "New Strife in Americus Mars Victim's Funeral," *Los Angeles Times*, August 1, 1965, in Leventhal, 67.

15. George Landry, "100 Troopers Are Patrolling in Americus," *Macon Telegraph*, July 29, 1965, in Leventhal, 500.

16. Bevan Johnstone, "Court Orders Women Freed," *Atlanta Constitution*, August 30, 1963, in Leventhal, 494.

17. "5 Negroes Beaten in Rights Picketing in Americus, Ga.," *New York Times*, August 1, 1965.

18. The Americus-Sumter County Movement Remembered Committee's plans include not only a museum, but also a "Living Heritage Walking Tour" that would stop at places significant to the movement. One planned stop is the Kwik Chek. Another stop is the Martin Theater. Americus-Sumter County Movement Remembered Committee.

19. "Rights Groups Rebuffed"; and "*Two Churches Bar Civil Rights Groups in Americus Drive*," *New York Times*, August 2, 1965, in Leventhal, *SCOPE of Freedom*, 498–99.

20. "Members Out on Bond," *UCLA Summer Bruin*, August 12, 1965, in Leventhal, 490.

21. George Landry, "Klansmen Stage Silent March in Americus," *Macon Telegraph*, August 9, 1965, in Leventhal, 222.

22. Landry, "*100 Troopers*," 500.

Chapter 6

1. For a detailed account of the tragic bombing and subsequent legal proceedings, see Jones, *Bending Toward Justice*; and Sikora, *Until Justice Rolls Down*.

2. See Theoharis, *Rebellious Life of Rosa Parks*; and Parks, *My Story*.

3. Lynn Goldsmith, "Diary of a Young Civil Rights Worker," Summer 1965, in Lynn Goldsmith Papers: The Diary and Papers of a Young Civil Rights Worker, Robert D. Farber University Archives and Special Collections, Brandeis

University, http://lts.brandeis.edu/research/archives-speccoll/exhibits/scope/diarytranscript.html. Goldsmith was a SCOPE volunteer who attended the SCLC annual convention in Birmingham. One of the comments in her diary was that the convention "was very concerned about the situation in Viet Nam."

4. Deppe, *Operation Breadbasket.*

5. See discussions of Dr. King and his position on the Vietnam War in Lewis, *King: A Biography*, 304–11; Smiley, *Death of a King*; and West, *Radical King.*

6. Bruce Hartford, "Civil Rights Movement History 1965: Selma & the March to Montgomery," CRMA, https://www.crmvet.org/tim/timhis65.htm; and Dittmer, *The Good Doctors.*

7. Hartford, "Civil Rights Movement History."

8. Hartford. See also Lewis, *King: A Biography*, 304.

9. "About Michael," Ráday Salon, https://www.radaysalon.org/about-michael.html.

10. Eig, *King*, 518–20. See also Lewis, *King: A Biography*, 359.

11. Hartford, "Civil Rights Movement History."

12. Lusane, *Black History of the White House*, 306; and Simmons, "About Michael."

13. *Bond v. Floyd*, 385 U.S. 116 (1966).

Chapter 7

1. SCOPE volunteer questionnaire responses (post-project), 1965, in Leventhal, *SCOPE of Freedom*, 171–83, where completed forms from several SCOPE volunteers are reproduced. Along with the survey form, each SCOPE volunteer received a form letter addressed "Dear SCOPE Volunteer" from Dr. King, thanking them for their service. Martin Luther King Jr., to SCOPE volunteers, October 1965, CRMA, https://www.crmvet.org/docs/6510_scope_mlk_letter.pdf.

2. SCLC, "The Results of Southern Christian Leadership Conference's 1965 Summer Community Organization and Political Education Project," 1965, CRMA, https://www.crmvet.org/docs/scope65.pdf.

3. R. T. Blackwell, "Memorandum to Dr. King and Rev. Abernathy," August 25, 1965, in Leventhal, *SCOPE of Freedom*, 92–93.

4. Carmichael, *Ready for Revolution*, 427.

5. In a later memorandum dated February 14, 1966, Blackwell wrote to Dr. King about "the conflict between myself and Mr. Williams." R. T. Blackwell, "A General Overview of S.C.L.C.," memorandum to Dr. Martin Luther King Jr., February 14, 1966, in Leventhal, *SCOPE of Freedom*, 111–14.

6. Hosea L. Williams, "Quarterly Report," memorandum to Dr. Martin Luther King Jr., November 6, 1965, in Leventhal, 95–103.

7. SCLC, "Results of Summer Community Project."

8. SCLC, "Results." The report also stated that SCOPE was responsible for giving national attention to Americus, Georgia.

9. Hosea Williams, transcript of Interview 0337_1, slides 1 and 2, Stanford University Special Collections and Archives, in Leventhal, *SCOPE of Freedom*, 122.

10. Williams, 120–38.

11. Williams, 123.

12. John Morris, "March in Capital Selects Slogans," *New York Times*, November 23, 1965, 14. There was also a full-page advertisement at page 28 of the *New York Times*, November 23, 1965, encouraging people to attend the march. It listed the sponsors, the speakers, and why the march was being held. "March on Washington: A Call to Mobilize the Conscience of America," *New York Times*, November 23, 1965, 28, advertisement.

13. Max Frankel, "Demonstrators Decorous—3 White House Aides Meet with Leaders," *New York Times*, November 27, 1965, 1.

14. "Throng of 20,000 Marches in Protest of Vietnam War," *Washington Post*, November 28, 1965.

15. "Throng of 20,000."

16. "Throng of 20,000."

17. "A Marcher for Peace," *New York Times*, November 27, 1965.

18. This was not the first time that Coretta King had spoken publicly about her opposition to the Vietnam War. In May 1965 she spoke at a conference at the Women's International League for Peace in Chicago, and in June 1965, at an antiwar rally at Madison Square Garden, where she was the only woman to speak. Eig, *King*, 447.

19. McAtee, *Transformed*, 202; and Dick Atlee, *Letters from Mississippi: Fall 1964 and Summer 1965*, https://dickatlee.com/issues/mississippi/pdfs/atlee_mississippi_letters.pdf.

Chapter 8

1. Eig, *King*, 225–27. See also Chicago Public Library, Woodson Regional Library, Vivian G. Harsh Research Collection of Afro-American History and Literature, "Chicago SNCC (Student Nonviolent Coordinating Committee) History Project Archives," https://www.chipubliclib.org/fa-chicago-sncc; and Carl Davidson, "Looking Back, Looking Forward: SNCC's 50th and the Ongoing Battle for Democracy," *Keep On Keepin' On . . .*, April 25, 2010, https://carldavidson.blogspot.com/2010/04/looking-back-looking-forward-sncc-50th.html.

2. *Boynton v. Virginia*, 364 U.S. 454 (1960).

3. See Oshinsky, *Worse Than Slavery*; and Taylor, *Down on Parchman Farm*.

4. See Eig, *King*, 375.

5. *Brown v. Board of Education*, 347 U.S. 483 (1954).

6. Linda Reed, "Mississippi Sovereignty Commission Spy Agency, 1956 –1977," *Between the Gate Posts*, April 5, 2012, https://betweenthegateposts.blogspot.com/2012/04/mississippi-sovereignty-commission-spy.html. A PBS documentary movie, *Spies of Mississippi*, directed by Dawn Porter (Trilogy Films, 2014) covers the Sovereignty Commission.

7. Carmichael, *Ready for Revolution*, 363.

8. See Blackstock, *Cointelpro*; and Weiner, *Enemies*.

9. Oppenheimer, "Mobs, Vigilantes, Cops, and Feds," 64.

10. Oppenheimer.

11. See Holsaert et al., *Hands on the Freedom Plow*, pt. 5.

12. Ling, "Half-Forgotten Dream." See also Eig, *King*, 426.

13. Carmichael, *Ready for Revolution*, 358.

14. Carmichael.

15. "Traveling in integrated cars through the South was suicidal," according to Maria Gitin in *This Bright Light of Ours* (175).

16. Bruce Hartford, "Civil Rights Movement History 1965: Selma & the March to Montgomery," CRMA, https://www.crmvet.org/tim/timhis65.htm

17. Hartford, "Civil Rights Movement History."

18. See Holsaert et al., *Hands on the Freedom Plow*, 387.

19. See Eig, *King*, 230–38. On May 4, 1960, Dr. King and his wife Coretta hosted Lillian Smith, a White writer who was undergoing treatment for cancer at Emory University Hospital, for dinner at their home in Atlanta. After dinner, King drove Smith back to the hospital. While driving with Smith, King was stopped by a police officer. King suspected that he was stopped because he was driving with a White woman. He had recently moved from Montgomery, Alabama, to Atlanta and still carried his Alabama driver's license, which was a violation of Georgia law. The police officer issued King a citation for driving without a valid license. Although at the time this encounter did not seem significant, it led to King's arrest and a national controversy that October, when King joined students at a sit-in at a snack bar at Rich's, a downtown Atlanta department store. The protest then moved to the Magnolia Room, a restaurant inside Rich's. When King and the other protesters refused to leave, all were arrested for trespass. Everyone, except King, was quickly released from jail, and charges were immediately dropped. King was held in jail, however, because of a probationary sentence he had received in the Georgia driver's license case in exchange for entering a guilty plea. The Georgia judge, ruling that King had violated the terms of his probation with his participation in the protest at Rich's, sentenced him to four months of hard labor in a public works camp, and denied bond pending an appeal. King's imprisonment led to requests for intervention to presidential candidates Richard Nixon and John Kennedy. Kennedy's willingness to help King get released from jail led King's father, Dr. King Sr., to switch his support from Nixon to Kennedy. Some believe that this switch of support was crucial to Kennedy's 1960 election victory.

Chapter 9

1. For a general discussion of racial segregation in Mississippi, see David H. Jackson Jr., "Segregation," July 11, 2017, last updated April 15, 2018, Center for the Study of Southern Culture, *Mississippi Encyclopedia*, http://mississippiencyclopedia.org/entries/segregation/.

2. See Lowe-Reid, "Discrimination."

3. McAtee, *Transformed*, 98–99.

4. This is just one of many comments from Ira Grupper that I have relied upon in writing this chapter. William McAtee also relied on Ira Grupper in his book *Transformed*. At the time I met with Ira, I was unaware of McAtee's book.

5. Grupper, "W. J. and Curtis." See also McAtee, *Transformed*, 202, 266.

6. See Holsaert et al., *Hands on the Freedom Plow*, pt. 5.

7. Marion Helland, "Freedom School, Voter Registration, Marches (AL, MS)," *CRMA*, last modified 2005, http://www.crmvet.org/vet/hellandm.htm.

8. "Bullets, Fire Riddle Columbia COFO Office," *Tupelo Journal*, author's copy.

9. "CR Headquarters Burns in Columbia," *Hattiesburg American*, July 1, 1965, http://newspaperarchive.com/hattiesburg-american/1965-07-31/page-1.

10. "Blaze Damages Home on Nathan," *Columbia-Progress*, August 5, 1965.

11. Ira Grupper, interview by Amber Duke, June 14, 2011, University of Louisville Oral History Center, https://ohc.library.louisville.edu/ohms/viewer.php?cachefile=2011_36_07_grupper.xml.

12. See Holsaert et al., *Hands on the Freedom Plow*, pt. 8.

13. The FBI program was known as COINTELPRO. See Church Committee, *FBI, COINTELPRO, and King.*

14. Romantic involvements among civil rights workers of different races were not uncommon. Disclosure of such relationships to those outside the movement were less common. See Watson, *Freedom Summer*, 231, quoting a White female civil rights worker during Freedom Summer in 1964: "I'm sure I wasn't the only white woman to fall in love with a Black man. I wrote home about a boyfriend but did not mention that he was Black."

Chapter 10

1. "Fact Sheet: Background on Greenville Refugees," University of Southern Mississippi Digital Collections, http://digilib.usm.edu; and Sue Thrasher, "Air Force Evicts Poor," *New South Student* 3, no. 2 (February 1966): 10, CRMA, https://www.crmvet.org/docs/6602_ssoc_nss-r.pdf.

2. See "Greenville Air Force Base Occupation," CRMA, https://www.crmvet.org/tim/timhis66.htm.

3. See Mississippi Freedom Democratic Party, *Memorandum*, February 10, 1966, http://didgilib.usm.edu.

4. "Commission on the Delta Ministry, *Delta Ministry Reports: Greenville Air Force Base—What Happened and Why*, Document #1C/S03.39 (February

1966). https://www.crmvet.org/docs/6602_dm_afb-c.pdf. See also Newman, *Divine Agitators.*

5. "Greenville Air Force Base Occupation."

6. Poor People's Conference, *statement from Greenville Air Force Base*, January 31, 1966, CRMA, https://www.crmvet.org/docs/660131_ppc_statement.pdf.

7. "Mississippi Air Base Occupied by Negroes in Search of Jobs," *New York Times*, February 1, 1966, 23.

8. "*Events at the Air Base,*" *Poverty and the Federal Government*, March 1966, https://www.crmvet.org/info/6603_poverty_liberation.pdf .

9. Gene Roberts, "Air Force Ejects Negroes Occupying a Mississippi Base," *New York Times*, February 2, 1966, 1.

10. *"Events at the Air Base," Poverty and the Federal Government.*

11. "Mississippi Air Base Occupied," 23.

12. Paul Mashburn, a member of the Air Police squad sent to evict the occupiers, wrote years later: "I remember some of the black protestors spitting on the black Air Police. I am very saddened by that." Jim Woodrick, "Greenville's Air Force Base," *And Speaking of Which . . .*, December 4, 2012, https://andspeakingofwhich.blogspot.com/2012/12/greenvilles-air-force-base.html.

13. A transcript of the press conference can be found at "The Background of the Greenville Air Base Live-In," *The Movement* 2, no. 3 (March 1966): 6, CRMA, https://www.crmvet.org/docs/mvmt/6603mvmt.pdf.

14. Thrasher, "Air Force Evicts Poor," 10.

15. Edward P. Moore, "Evicted Squatters Await Next Move in Greenville Row: Screaming Demonstrators Curse, Bite Air Police and Threaten Prompt Return Despite Concessions," *New York Times*, February 2, 1966.

16. "Mississippi Air Base Occupied," 23.

17. Roberts, "Air Force Ejects Negroes," 23.

18. For many civil rights workers, being arrested and spending time in jail was viewed as a badge of honor. See Holsaert et al., *Hands on the Freedom Plow*, 373. Stokely Carmichael took a different position: "We're not here to go to jail. We're here to do a job. Which cannot be done in a cell. Your duty is to stay out of jail if at all possible, okay?" Carmichael, *Ready for Revolution*, 386.

19. "Deal with this problem expeditiously and directly through surplus food distribution, crash employment programs, and as many poverty programs as we can fund. If we do not do this, there is a real possibility that Mississippi will be Selma, Alabama of 1966." "Greenville Air Force Base Occupation."

20. Woodrick, "Greenville's Air Force Base."

Chapter 11

1. Lawrence Bush, "Mississippi Freedom Summer—Fifty Years Later, Part Two," *Jewish Currents*, June 14, 2014, https://jewishcurrents.org/mississippi-freedom-summer-fifty-years-later-part-two.

2. See Holsaert et al., *Hands on the Freedom Plow*, pt. 10.

3. Stokely Carmichael, "What We Want," *New York Review of Books*, September 22, 1966, 5–6.

4. Bond, "SNCC: What We Did."

5. Oppenheimer, "Mobs, Vigilantes, Cops, and Feds," 64.

6. See Meredith, *Three Years in Mississippi*; and McGee, *James Meredith*.

7. See Wallach, "Replicating History." See also Varela, "Time to Get Ready"; and Bush, "Mississippi Freedom Summer."

8. Joseph, *Stokely*, 167–68; and Holsaert et al., *Hands on the Freedom Plow*, 324.

9. In 1967 the organization's name was changed to Student National (not Nonviolent) Coordinating Committee.

10. See Farmer, *Lay Bare the Heart*.

11. *Loving v. Virginia*, 388 U.S. 1 (1967)

12. No one in the family ever met Curtis or knew anything about him other than that he was a Black man. I don't think anyone knew his name. If his existence was ever mentioned, and I do not recall any such mention, it would have been only as Iris's daughter's father. No one knew that Iris and Curtis had been legally married. It was assumed they were not. Perhaps there was some thought that they may have gone through some sort of marriage ceremony in Mississippi that had no legal validity. No one knew that Curtis was living in Philadelphia for many years. In short, we knew nothing about him, and no one asked. By the time I learned about Curtis from Iris, he had been dead for almost twenty years. In 1996, at the age of fifty-nine, Curtis died of natural causes. Ira Grupper was contacted by Curtis's second wife and informed of his death. Curtis and Ira had kept in touch over the years, and Ira attended the funeral in Philadelphia and gave the eulogy for Curtis. Curtis is buried in a cemetery just outside Philadelphia.

Epilogue

1. Maria Gitin writes that when she was talking about her experiences with a fellow civil rights worker, "forty years of suppressed feeling spilled into tears." Others had similar experiences: "Other parents had disowned their children, and many vets went years without talking about their time in the movement." Gitin, *This Bright Light of Ours*, 175.

2. Boyd Faust died on May 22, 2022, at the age of seventy-eight. I was fortunate to have met and interviewed him in Houston, Texas, in June 2016. We discussed the time he spent with the civil rights movement in the 1960s, and he provided me with detailed typed notes, printed emails and blog posts, and news clippings that he had compiled over the years. I suspect that at one point he was considering writing about his experiences. To my knowledge, he never did. I learned about his death when he stopped responding to my emails, and I searched for his obituary. I found it on the website of the Strickland Funeral

Homes, www.stricklandfuneralhomes.com/obituaries/RevBoyd-Faust. The obituary included that "as a young man, he was heavily involved as an advocate for equality in the Civil Rights Movement." Faust was ordained at Grace Lutheran Church in Teaneck, New Jersey. He served congregations in Chicago, North Dakota, and Texas, and went on many missions to Africa. He was married in 2005. Faust and Iris saw each other in 2015 at the fiftieth SCOPE reunion in Atlanta.

3. I interviewed Ira Grupper at his home in Louisville, Kentucky, in July 2016. He seemed to remember every detail about his time with the civil rights movement. Unlike Iris, Ira was often asked about his experiences, and he was always willing to share his stories. He never mentioned Iris to anyone. He wrote columns for newspapers and organization newsletters. Despite not having a college degree, he taught classes on civil rights at Bellarmine University in Louisville, Kentucky. He did numerous oral history interviews recounting his experiences in the civil rights movement. See, for example, Ira Grupper, interview by Amber Duke, June 14, 2011, University of Louisville Oral History Center, https://ohc.library.louisville.edu/ohms/viewer.php?cachefile=2011_36_07_grupper.xml. Ira was interviewed by William McAtee for his book *Transformed*, in which he is named in the dedication. Ira was generous with his time with me and always responded quickly to my requests. As I worked through my research and eventual writing of this book, I often emailed Ira for clarification or comment. At first he responded quickly, but after a while it would be weeks before I heard back from him. In one email, he told me that his health was declining; he was having trouble reading and concentrating. Not long thereafter, I found his obituary during a Google search. Ira died at the age of eighty in July 2024. The online obituary written by his children stated that his days with SNCC in Atlanta, Hattiesburg, and Columbia "were the proudest days of his life." He had spent his entire life involved in "advocacy work for civil rights, disability rights, and labor rights," and "stood up for people facing injustice." He was described as "a proud troublemaker and ungovernable character," who was "standing ready to make good trouble." The obituary can be found by searching "Ira Grupper" on https://www.legacy.com.

4. For more information on Michael Simmons, his personal website is www.msimmons.org. See also Michael Simmons, "A Life in the Struggle: SNCC & Radical Black Internationalism," Paul Robeson House and Museum Parlor Talk, October 2, 2021, Making Worlds Bookstore, https://www.makingworldsbooks.org/events/michael-simmons-sncc-amp-radical-black-internationalism.

5. Despite his extensive discussion of events in 1966 in Columbia, Mississippi, including detailed descriptions of the activities of Ira Grupper, Curtis Styles, and W. J. McClenton, Iris is not named in McAtee's book, *Transformed*. The closest mention I found of her is on page 184, where there is a discussion

of a meeting between Mayor McLean and "Willis McClenton and one white girl" on July 25, 1966. This unidentified "white girl" is almost certainly Iris.

6. W. J. McClenton died in January 2002 at the age of seventy-three. He lived his entire life in Columbia, Mississippi, and remained active in the civil rights movement with the Marion County chapter of the SCLC. Besides working as a truck driver, he helped people with their appeals of disability claim denials. Ira Grupper gave a eulogy at his funeral at the Friendship Missionary Baptist Church outside Columbia. Ira called W.J. his "friend," his "brother," "a good person." See McAtee, *Transformed*, 266.

7. SNCC Legacy Project, www.sncclegacyproject.org. The SNCC Legacy Project was funded by the Andrew Mellon Foundation to support the study of SNCC's history. See also the website www.onevotesncc.org, which "documents how the bottom-up strategies of young people and black community leaders across the Deep South created an expansion of political, social and economic opportunity for all citizens in the 1960's."

8. Meg Kinnard, "Civil Rights Leader Softens on Sanders," *Baltimore Sun*, February 14, 2016. See also Carl Davidson, "Looking Back, Looking Forward: SNCC's 50th and the Ongoing Battle for Democracy," *Keep On Keepin' On...*, April 25, 2010, https://carldavidson.blogspot.com/2010/04/looking-back-looking-forward-sncc-50th.html. Davidson, a former SNCC staff member, wrote that it was "ordinary people" who were the base of the movement.

BIBLIOGRAPHY

Alter, Jonathan. *His Very Best: Jimmy Carter, a Life*. New York: Simon & Schuster, 2020.

Anderson, Jose Felipe. *Genius for Justice: Charles Hamilton Houston and the Reform of American Law*. Durham, NC: Carolina Academic Press, 2021.

Belfrage, Sally. *Freedom Summer*. Charlottesville: University of Virginia Press, 1990.

Blackstock, Nelson. *Cointelpro: The FBI's Secret War on Political Freedom*. New York: Pathfinder Press, 1975.

Bond, Julian. "SNCC: What We Did." *Monthly Review* 52, no. 5 (October 2000). https://www.monthlyreview.org/2000/10/01/sncc-what-we did.

Brooks, Meagan Parker, and Davis W. Horick, eds. *The Speeches of Fannie Lou Hamer: To Tell It Like It Is*. Jackson: University Press of Mississippi, 2010.

Brooks, Meagan Parker. *Fannie Lou Hamer: America's Freedom Fighting Woman*. Lanham, MD: Rowman & Littlefield, 2020.

Cagin, Seth. *We Are Not Afraid: The Story of Goodman, Schwerner, and Chaney and the Civil Rights Campaign for Mississippi*. New York: Macmillan, 1988.

Carmichael, Stokely (Kwame Ture). *Ready for Revolution: The Life and Struggles of Stokely Carmichael*. With Ekwueme Michael Thelwell. New York: Scribner, 2005.

Carson, Clayborne. *In Struggle: SNCC and the Black Awakening of the 1960s*. Cambridge, MA: Harvard University Press, 1981.

Church Committee. *The FBI, COINTELPRO, and Martin Luther King, Jr.: Final Report of the Select Committee to Study Governmental Operations with Respect to Intelligence*. Gainesville, FL: Red and Black, 2011.

Dean, John. *Blind Ambition*. New York: Simon & Schuster, 1976.

Dennis, David, Jr., and David Dennis Sr. *The Movement Made Us: A Father, a Son, and the Legacy of a Freedom Ride*. New York: Harper, 2022.

Deppe, Martin L. *Operation Breadbasket: An Untold Story of Civil Rights in Chicago, 1966–1971*. Athens: University of Georgia Press, 2017.

Dittmer, John. *The Good Doctors: The Medical Committee for Human Rights and the Struggle for Social Justice in Health Care*. Jackson: University Press of Mississippi, 2017.

———. *Local People: The Struggle for Civil Rights in Mississippi*. Urbana: University of Illinois Press, 1994.

Eig, Jonathan. *King: A Life*. New York: Farrar, Straus & Giroux, 2023.

Farmer, James. *Lay Bare the Heart: An Autobiography of the Civil Rights Movement*. Fort Worth, TX: TCU Press, 1998.

Foner, Eric. *A Short History of Reconstruction*. New York: Harper & Row, 1990.

Franklin, V. P. *The Young Crusaders: The Untold Story of the Children and Teenagers Who Galvanized the Civil Rights Movement*. Boston: Beacon Press, 2021.

Gates, Henry Louis Jr. *The Black Church: This Is Our Story, This Is Our Song*. New York: Penguin Press, 2021.

Gitin, Maria. *This Bright Light of Ours: Stories from the Voting Rights Fight*. Tuscaloosa: University of Alabama Press, 2014.

Grupper, Ira. "W.J. and Curtis." *FORsooth*, March 2002. https://dickatlee.com/issues/mississippi/pdfs/labor_paeans_0203.pdf.

Holsaert, Faith, Martha Prescod Norman Noonan, Judy Richardson, Betty Garman Robinson, Jean Smith Young, and Dorothy M. Zellner, eds. *Hands on the Freedom Plow: Personal Accounts by Women in SNCC*. Urbana: University of Illinois Press, 2010.

Jones, Doug. *Bending Toward Justice: The Birmingham Church Bombing That Changed the Course of Civil Rights*. New York: All Point Books, 2019.

Joseph, Peniel E. *Stokely: A Life*. New York: Basic Civitas Books, 2014.

———. *The Sword and the Shield: The Revolutionary Lives of Malcolm X and Martin Luther King, Jr*. New York: Basic Books, 2020.

Katagiri, Yasuhiro. *The Mississippi State Sovereignty Commission: Civil Rights and States' Rights*. Jackson: University Press of Mississippi, 2001.

Leventhal, Willy Siegel. *The SCOPE of Freedom: The Leadership of Hosea Williams with Dr. King's Summer '65 Student Volunteers*. Montgomery, AL: Challenge Press, 2005.

Lewis, David Levering. *King: A Biography*. 3rd ed. Urbana: University of Illinois Press, 2012.

Lewis, John. *Across That Bridge*. New York: Hachette, 2012.

———. *Walking with the Wind: A Memoir of the Movement*. New York: Simon & Schuster, 1998.

Ling, Peter. "Martin Luther King's Half-Forgotten Dream." *History Today* 48, no. 4 (April 1998). https://www.historytoday.com/archive/martin-luther-king%E2%80%99s-half-forgotten-dream.

Loewen, James W. *Sundown Towns: A Hidden Dimension of American Racism*. New York: New Press, 2005.

Lowe-Reid, Lillie. "Discrimination and the Civil Rights Movement: My Personal Struggles." *FORsooth*, February 2009. https://louisvillefor.org/wp-content/uploads/2014/11/for-2-09.pdf.

Lusane, Clarence. *The Black History of the White House*. San Francisco: City Lights, 2011.

McAdam, Doug. *Freedom Summer*. New York: Oxford University Press, 1988.

McAtee, William. *Transformed: A White Mississippi Pastor's Journey into Civil Rights and Beyond*. Jackson: University Press of Mississippi, 2011.

McGee, Meredith Coleman. *James Meredith: Warrior and the America That Created Him*. Santa Barbara, CA: Praeger, 2013.

McWhirter, Cameron. *Red Summer: The Summer of 1919 and the Awakening of Black America*. New York: Henry Holt, 2011.

Meacham, Jon. *His Truth Is Marching On*. New York: Random House, 2020.

Meredith, James. *Three Years in Mississippi*. Jackson: University Press of Mississippi, 2019.

Meyers, Allen. *Oxford Circle: The Jewish Community of Northeast Philadelphia*. Charleston, SC: Arcadia, 2004.

Newman, Mark. *Divine Agitators: The Delta Ministry and Civil Rights in Mississippi*. Athens: University of Georgia Press, 2004.

Oppenheimer, Martin. "Mobs, Vigilantes, Cops, and Feds: The Repression of the Student Nonviolent Coordinating Committee." *New Politics* 14 (Summer 2012): 64.

Oshinsky, David M. *Worse Than Slavery: Parchman Farm and the Ordeal of Jim Crow Justice*. New York: Simon & Schuster, 1996.

Parks, Rosa. *My Story*. New York: Turtleback Books, 1999.

Payne, Charles M. *I've Got the Light of Freedom: The Organizing Tradition and the Mississippi Freedom Struggle*. Berkeley: University of California Press, 1995.

Preacely, Peggy Trotter Dammond. "It Was Simply in My Blood." In *Hands on the Freedom Plow: Personal Accounts by Women in SNCC*, edited by Faith S. Holsaert, Martha Prescod Norman Noonan, Judy Richardson, Betty Garman Robinson, Jean Smith Young, and Dorothy M. Zellner, 373–76. Urbana: University of Illinois Press, 2010.

Ransby, Barbara. *Ella Baker and the Black Freedom Movement: A Radical Democratic Vision*. Chapel Hill: University of North Carolina Press, 2003.

Reed, Lesley-Anne Stafford. "Smells Like Money: The Rise and Fall of a Paper Dream in Dixie, 1920–1975." PhD diss., University of Georgia, 2012. https://openscholar.uga.edu/record/9949334146602959.

Rice, Rolundus R. *Hosea Williams, A Lifetime of Defiance and Protest*. Columbia: University of South Carolina Press, 2021.

Rochvarg, Arnold. *Watergate Victory: Mardian's Appeal*. Lanham, MD: University Press of America, 1995.

Schultz, Debra L. *Going South: Jewish Women in the Civil Rights Movement*. New York: NYU Press, 2001.

Sikora, Frank. *Until Justice Rolls Down: The Birmingham Church Bombing Case*. Tuscaloosa: University of Alabama Press, 1991.

Smiley, Tavis. *Death of a King*. New York: Little, Brown, 2014.

Sorin, Gretchen. *Driving While Black: African American Travel and the Road to Civil Rights*. New York: Liveright, 2020.

Sugarman, Tracy. *We Had Sneakers, They Had Guns: The Kids Who Fought for Civil Rights in Mississippi*. Syracuse, NY: Syracuse University Press, 2009.

Taylor, William Banks. *Down on Parchman Farm: The Great Prison in the Mississippi Delta*. Columbus: Ohio State University Press, 1999.

Theoharis, Jeanne. *The Rebellious Life of Mrs. Rosa Parks*. Boston: Beacon Press, 2015.

Todd, Lisa Anderson. *For a Voice and the Vote: My Journey with the Mississippi Freedom Democratic Party*. Lexington: University Press of Kentucky, 2015.

Toplin, Robert Brent. *History by Hollywood: The Use and Abuse of the Hollywood Past*. Urbana: University of Illinois Press, 1996.

Tuck, Stephen G. N. *Beyond Atlanta: The Struggle for Racial Equality in Georgia, 1940–1980*. Athens: University of Georgia Press, 2001.

Ture, Kwame, and Charles V. Hamilton. *Black Power: The Politics of Liberation*. New York: Random House, 1967.

Tyson, Timothy B. *The Blood of Emmett Till*. New York: Simon & Schuster, 2017.

Varela, Maria. "Time to Get Ready." In *Hands on the Freedom Plow: Personal Accounts by Women in SNCC*, edited by Faith S. Holsaert, Martha Prescod Norman Noonan, Judy Richardson, Betty Garman Robinson, Jean Smith Young, and Dorothy M. Zellner, 552–572. Urbana: University of Illinois Press, 2010.

Wallach, Jennifer Jensen. "Replicating History in a Bad Way? White Activists and Black Power in SNCC's Arkansas Project." *The Arkansas Historical Quarterly* 67, no. 3 (Autumn 2008): 268–287.

Wallach, Jennifer Jensen, and John A. Kirk, eds. *Arsnick: SNCC in Arkansas*. Fayetteville: University of Arkansas Press, 2011.

Watson, Bruce. *Freedom Summer: The Savage Season of 1964 That Made Mississippi Burn and Made America a Democracy*. New York: Viking Books, 2010.

Weiner, Tim. *Enemies: A History of the FBI*. New York: Random House, 2012.

West, Cornel, ed. *The Radical King*. Boston: Beacon Press, 2015.

INDEX

M

N